JN133124

Guide to the Temple Garden of Philosophy

Edited by
Rainer Schulzer

東洋大学出版会

Guide to the Temple Garden of Philosophy
Rainer Schulzer

Original English edition is published by Toyo University Press.
5-28-20 Hakusan, Bunkyo-ku, Tokyo 112-8606

PRINTED IN JAPAN

Here on every simile you ride to every truth. Here all being's words and word-shrines spring open for you; here all being wants to become word, all becoming wants to learn speech from you.

—Thus Spoke Zarathustra

Contents

I. Inoue Enryo's Guide to the Temple Garden of Philosophy

II. Introducing the World Sages

Appendix

Preface and Acknowledgments

This book is a revised and enlarged edition of the manuscript I published online, in 2017, in the fifth issue of *International Inoue Enryo Research*. Besides various corrections, the main changes made for the print edition are additions of illustrations, historical photographs, and recommendations for further reading. The photographs mainly serve to bridge the gap between the condition of the Garden in 1915, when Inoue Enryō's guidebook was first printed, and today. The pictures do not of course render a visit of the Garden obsolete. For those interested, but unable to visit Tokyo, it should be mentioned that Google Street View allows one to roam through the Garden. There are also introductory videos in English on the homepage of the park.

Inoue Enryō (1858–1919) thought of his garden as a pantheon of world philosophy where a visitor might learn about various thinkers, sages, and cultural heroes from India, Europe, and East Asia. Enryō's introductory texts about the individual sages, however, mostly resonate orthodox heroization instead of being based on critical historical research. In order to mitigate this circumstance, I point the reader to further resources (online, whenever possible) in the hope that the Temple Garden of Philosophy might indeed inspire a Western visitor to learn more about the rich philosophical heritage of the Chinese and Indian cultural spheres.

井上圓了

About sixty percent of this book is based on English translations produced by Inoue Genichi (1887–1972),

井上玄一

Enryō's son. Genichi's several attempts to publish an English guide to his father's Garden span almost forty years. The fragments he bequeathed are of different origins and varying quality. I edited, revised, and made use of these fragments as much as possible before complementing them with my own translations and editorial comments (see Editorial Notes). The result is a patchwork of English styles and translation methods for which I must apologize to the reader. Joseph M. LOGAN (Essential Lay Buddhism Study Center) did his best to revise the heterogeneous textual elements to become a readable whole. I am deeply thankful for his highly professional and conscientious help.

At the age of seventy-five, Genichi—who spoke about the "internationalization" of his father's Garden as his "life's work"—made his last attempt to finish his Guide in preparation for the 1964 Tokyo Olympics. Surely he would be gratified to see the Guide being finally published in time for the upcoming 2020 Tokyo Olympics. I desired, as well, to have this work published in 2019 as a way to commemorate the one-hundred-year anniversary of Inoue Enryō's death. And unfortunately, this timing has taken on additional significance in that Genichi's son, INOUE Tamio (1919–2019), Enryō's grandchild, who was born in the same year that Enryō died, passed away one hundred years later on the 8th of April of this year.

井上民雄

The publication of this book was made possible thanks to the 2018 Inoue Enryo Memorial Publication Grant awarded by Toyo University Press. Most of the photographs reproduced here, and all textual source materials on which this guide is based, are kept by the Inoue Enryo Research Center of Toyo University. I feel deeply grateful to the center's administration, and in particular to IIMURA Keiko, for supporting my research for many years. During the course of my research on the Temple Garden of Philosophy, I received generous and competent help from IDENO Naoki, of the Inoue Enryo Research Center, and from KITADA Kenji, the man behind the Inoue Enryo Memorial Museum of Toyo University. For helping me with Chinese inscriptions in the Garden, I am indebted to my friend ZHÀO Déwěi. The woodblock print shown on the cover of this book is from 1934, by the artist KOIZUMI Kishio (1893–1945). It was reproduced through the courtesy of its owner, IKEGAMI Masao (Toyo University). For the permission to use the souvenir stamps of the Temple Garden of Philosophy for this guide, I want to express my gratitude to the Park Administration, and particularly to KONISHI Rumiko, the member of this very friendly and always considerate team who created the stamps. Several pictures reproduced in this guide are owned by the Nakano History Museum and have only been digitalized at my request. I am deeply grateful to the museum director, Dr. HIDAI Katsuhito, and to KITAGAWA Naoko for their cooperation and their efforts. Last but not least, I want to thank Ilmer Thies Architects (Zürich/Berlin) for their kind help with the illustrations and the map that is included in this book.

飯村桂子
出野尚紀
北田健二
趙徳偉
小泉癸巳男
池上正男
小西留美子
比田井克仁
北河直子

Rainer Schulzer
April, 2019

Introduction to the English Edition by Inoue Genichi (1925)

Taking advantage of the pleasure hours of my weekends in New York City, I sought to study the ways and habits of American life. These studies were pursued with a view to aiding me in the further development of my work managing *Tetsugaku-dō*, or, as I have translated it into English, the Temple Garden of Philosophy.[1] I had been told that the atmosphere of this Temple in Tokyo was, to a great extent, reminiscent of the spiritual and intellectual environment of Concord, Massachusetts, and I therefore keenly desired to visit that place.

哲學堂

It was on a serene autumn day, in the year 1922, that I first visited the home of the great American thinker, Ralph Waldo Emerson. Through the good will and courtesy of Edward L. Emerson, the philosopher's son, I was given an opportunity to spend an entire day in tranquil meditation among scenes pervaded by the spirit of the Sage of Concord.

The school of philosophy, with which Emerson's name and fame are associated, now stands solitary and deserted among the fallen leaves—an almost forgotten dream, without a master. The nearby pine trees and crystal-clear brook give an air of spiritual serenity, reminding me of

1 Although Enryō himself used the word "public garden" or "park" 公園 in relation to his Garden (Ideno 2012), the precinct has been called "Park of the Philosophy Shrine" 哲學堂公園 in public only since 1946 (Miura 2002). Before I discovered Genichi's drafts, I had, coincidentally, translated 哲學堂公園 in the same way as Genichi rendered 哲學堂, namely, Temple Garden of Philosophy.

my father's Temple Garden of Philosophy. But is not this sacred spot of bygone philosophers losing its true spirit and influence? Most sightseers, bred in the materialistic environment of today, bestow but hasty and superficial glances upon this fragment of a sanctuary that should be an inspiration to Americans from generation to generation. Why is it, I mused, that the spiritual influence of the Concord philosopher is not stronger among his own countrymen of today? It would almost seem that, in the present state of American civilization, the transcendental philosophy of Emerson appeals more to the Oriental mind than to the Occidental one.

Japan owes much to America for opening her doors to Western civilization and liberating her from her self-imposed isolation. Since that time, an acquaintance with Western civilization has led to amazing advances in Japan in scientific research and in industrial development. But, on the other hand, the essence of Oriental civilization, with its idealistic trend, has not become much known to the Occidental world; certainly it has not affected the daily life of the people of the Western nations.

小泉八雲

It is true that Lafcadio HEARN (known in Japan as KOIZUMI Yakumo), and also Professor Ernest F. FENOLLOSA (my father's friend and instructor), did much toward interpreting the spirit of Japan and Japanese art for the Western world. They painted fascinating pictures; but even those pictures did not tempt the Western world to infuse the culture of the East into its life. Except as it holds out promises of commercial advantages, and as its military potential arouses apprehensive interest, Japan remains a country of mysticism, poetry, and romance to the people of the Occident.

It is not possible to understand Japan merely by skimming over its surfaces. The peculiarities of the language make an understanding of the life and spirit of the Japanese people difficult for Westerners. It is even more difficult for them to understand Oriental philosophy and its effect upon the people: it flows as a profound undercurrent through the Japanese mind, and it is key to solving the mysteries in any phase of national life. The Temple Garden of Philosophy is pervaded by a genuine Oriental spirit sprung from the particular interpretations and aspirations of my father. It appears small when measured according to American enterprise, but, in its method of expressing Oriental culture, it is unique.

There are those who criticize my father's philosophy, maintaining that he seemed to stray from the paths of philosophical science into those of dogmatism in the efforts of his last years, and that, to the curious, his Temple Garden of Philosophy appeals merely as a novelty. These critics have failed to see the true aspects of his idealistic striving. His philosophy may not be a philosophy in the technical sense of the word, and, as far as I know, it is different from modern philosophy; but we must remember that he was inspired by the noblest of ideals and strove to express the lofty promptings of his spirit.

My father thought that a man should develop the public or social elements in his nature to the maximum, and the private to the minimum—and that such a development should be natural for the public official because of his position. The independent citizen, however, should develop the public element of his character to the maximum of his own free will. Further, my father felt that men of moderate means, and those of large wealth as well, should, after adequate provision has been made for their families, give their surplus back to the public from which it originally came. Such public activities of the individual, and such public use of capital, were cardinal beliefs of my father. He has given concrete expression to these beliefs by means of the Temple Garden of Philosophy.

Even though my father may be criticized as a philosopher, he must be highly esteemed as a world educator. In Oriental philosophy we have the term *tetsugaku-sha* (philosophic scholar), signifying "philosopher" with its usual meaning, and the word *tetsu-jin* (philosophic man), signifying, to use my father's words, "world educator" or "practitioner of philosophy." In order to express this latter meaning, I have used words such as "sage," "wise man," "philosopher-saint," and "world educator" throughout this translation. It is only when this second meaning is taken into consideration that the Temple Garden of Philosophy can be rightly valued. Therefore, I particularly emphasize the Garden's mission of helping in the creation of world educators. When a genius among them appears, he will found a real philosophical religion. My father had hoped to found it, but he was only a pioneer. To accomplish his aim, I think that an exhaustive comparative study of Eastern and Western philosophies is of utmost importance. According to this interpretation of my father's ideas, I now plan the developments that follow.

哲學者

哲人

The building containing my father's collection of curios is to be enlarged into a Philosophical Museum. The library containing Buddhist, Chinese, and Japanese classical literature will be made to be even more extensive; it will be known as the Philosophical Library. On an adjoining tract of land, I hope to establish another garden—an outer garden. In this new garden, there will be symbols of modern developments in realism and religious feeling that contrast with my father's symbolic representations of the ideas of philosophy. These ideas may be expressed by laying out a garden according to a considered color scheme made vibrant by variety in plants and trees. An Oriental Society for Philosophical Research will also be founded to study Oriental philosophy from an international point of view, and to work in cooperation with Oriental Associations in all parts of the world.[2]

These ideas of future expansion, which may take time to realize, have been born out of my experiences while living in New York City, the cosmopolitan city of the world, and by a study of its gigantic educational enterprises of international scope.

In the course of my studies at Colombia University, I frequently mentioned the Temple Garden of Philosophy. I was advised by my instructor, Miss Kate B. MILLER, to translate this guidebook into English in order to interest Americans in the work. Thus encouraged, I have translated this little book with the help of Miss Miller and my private instructor, Miss Charlotte FRIETCH—who both understand the Japanese mind. Although my translation has been revised by them, they have kept the tone of my father and the garden, which is to me of far greater importance than the reality of either. I wish also to thank Mr. Henry W. TAFT, president of the Japan Society in New York City, and Mrs. Arlene W. ADAMS, Vice President of the Japan Society in Boston, for their helpful suggestions in preparing this book.

Much of my work was carried out in the delightfully harmonious home of Mr. and Mrs. Charles LE SASSIER, which is situated in a wooded section of Navesink

2 Genichi was unfortunately not able to realize his plans.

Highlands, New Jersey, overlooking the vast Atlantic Ocean, beyond the picturesque peninsula of Sandy Hook. This area seemed to me to be a Western replica of the pine grove on Miho peninsula on the Pacific Ocean side of Japan. The idyllic scenery and the congenial family life proved to be both admirable and idealistically suited to my work. These conditions have been greatly conducive to the successful accomplishment of my task.

三保

I wish therefore, to express my deep gratitude to these friends for the valuable aid they have given me in furthering the publication of this volume as a first step towards the internationalization of my father's ideal, with the hope that the East and West will meet some day in perfect understanding.

Inoue Genichi
June 6, 1925
Sixth anniversary of my father's death
Navesink Highlands, New Jersey

Preface by Inoue Genichi (1920)

The Temple Garden of Philosophy was established by my father, the late Doctor Inoue Enryō, as a work of his later years—subsequent to his retirement from the Philosophy Academy (today's "Oriental College," or Toyo University). The plan and design of this temple were quite original, and it is for this reason that I can, even to this day, divine his mood and mind as a living spirit which steps forth from this creation of his to meet and greet me.

哲學館
東洋大学

To understand his creation, one must know certain aspects of his character. He declared that he valued the jewel and the stone equally. An artist may consider my father's symbolic representations of philosophical ideas inconsistent with true art. Such a criticism would not touch the real value of his work, which is truly an expression of his character. He was a man of great initiative, both as a philosopher and a businessman. Hence, in this unique creation we discern, if not the artistic notes, the unusual blending of the transcendent tones of the philosopher and the practical achievement of the man of business.

The Temple Garden of Philosophy was originally established through his own contributions. He acquired funds for this purpose by the sale of his calligraphies at moderate prices, ranging from fifty pence (Jp. *sen*) to ten yen. Half of the sum thus gained was contributed to the Temple, together with private holdings accumulated by means of his thrift. The remaining half acquired by the

錢

sale of his ideograph compositions was denoted to local public works.

In order to accomplish his gigantic task, he was obliged to give a total of 5,503 lectures in 54 cities, 481 counties, and 2,261 villages and towns—2,796 places in all, covering a period of twelve years, dating from 1906 to 1918 (statistics covering the work of 1919 are not included herein)—to a total audience of 1,378,675 individuals. I have no definite knowledge as to what influence my father's lectures may have exercised upon the people; I do know, however, that he cherished the hope of making them understand Japan's national ethics. He exerted himself to the utmost to achieve this end, working ceaselessly with an indefatigable energy.

大連

It was in the year 1919, when he was on his way back to Japan, having completed a lecturing tour in China, that he suddenly fell ill during a lecture at a Dàlián kindergarten (from Russ. Dal'nii). This illness proved fatal, for he passed away in the early dawn of the following day, June 6th, 1919, taking his last breath in the school where he had been lecturing only the day before. It might thus seem that his innermost desire was granted, inasmuch as he had hoped death would find him in the midst of his glorious task.

岡田良平
金子恭輔

In his last will, he provided for the permanence of the Temple Garden of Philosophy by leaving property approximating 500,000 yen in value for that purpose. Accordingly, the Temple Garden of Philosophy Foundation was chartered by the Minister of Education on December 9, 1919. Under this charter, the management is in the hands of three directors: Okada Ryōhei, my father's friend, Kaneko Kyōsuke, my brother-in-law, and me. It is gratifying, therefore, to realize that the will of my father will be carried out in accordance with his most cherished wishes.

As one of the directors, I wish to see forth the spirit and purpose of the Temple Garden of Philosophy. Rather than for scholars who live their lives in books, it is intended for the common people—to enable them to understand and realize principles of philosophy in their lives.

On the temple grounds we find a library comprising some forty thousand ancient volumes. However, this vast collection of books was only a means to an end, for after he had thoroughly read and digested this ancient literature, he cast it aside and faced the living truth of a living world. In one of his own books we find a passage that vividly pictures an experience of his youth that dominated his later life. It goes as follows:

> In ascending Eminent Summit Mountain 比叡山 (Mt. Hiei) one day, I discovered to my surprise that but few pilgrims seemed to be intent upon making the ascent. Another mountain, Mount Highplain 高野山 (Mt. Kōya), was greatly frequented and generally crowded with mountain climbers. The former is situated near Kyoto, the ancient capital of Japan, whereas the latter is located in a remoter section of the country, distant from that city. Why then, we may well ask, should the pilgrimage to one of the mountains be so popular, while that to the other was so uncommon? It appeared that this strange circumstance was wholly dependent upon the individual characteristics of the holy men who had opened up the paths to these two mountains, and to the temples erected on their summits. The temple which is located on the top of Eminent Summit Mountain was founded by the Great Teacher Transmitting the Teaching 傳教大師, or Saichō 最澄 (Utmost Clarity), and the one on Mount Highplain was founded by the Great Teacher Spreading the Dharma 弘法大師, or Kūkai 空海 (Sea of Emptiness). Although these two priests were contemporaries, and both of them knew equal fame, Saichō, on the one hand,

as the Emperor's adviser, kept himself aloof from the public at large, whereas Kūkai wandered through the country exerting all his efforts towards the uplifting of the lower classes. For this reason, Saichō's merits are today acknowledged but by the few, while Kūkai's praises are constantly sung, and his great benevolence is never forgotten. Arrogant as it may appear to compare myself to these famed sages, it would be my desire to emulate the virtues of Kūkai rather than those of Saichō.

Inspiration derived from that early experience dominated my father's entire life. Therefore, if those who visit the Temple Garden are to grasp the living spirit of my father that dwells therein, it is important for them to bear in mind that, because of his unselfish devotion to his democratic ideals, he gave himself wholly to the service of the common good.

It may be said that while my father looked upon the priest Kūkai with great reverence, he also held Herbert SPENCER, the English philosopher, in high esteem. At the time he was sojourning in England some years ago, he was profoundly moved at the sight of the simple tomb of this renowned philosopher in the midst of the common people, as was befitting of a simple scholar who scorned titles and rank. It was my father's intention to found a philosophy—as Herbert SPENCER had done—upon completing his countrywide wandering in Japan; a plan that came to naught, owing to his unexpected and sudden death. There is no need, however, to lament this circumstance, since my father's mission as a scholar belonged to the past, and had its climax in the period of enlightenment, the philosophic renaissance of Japan. His mission as a philosopher-saint—as the Sage of Wadayama (Peaceful Paddy Hill)—has no end. Had he lived on and continued his education of the people, would his influence have

和田山

FIGURE 1. Mount Fuji seen from the Temple Garden of Philosophy

been more far-reaching and effective than it will be now as it emanates from the Temple Garden of Philosophy, his living masterpiece and fit crystallization of his spirit?

His last poem, composed at the Great Wall of China, and written just before his death, is very suggestive of his noble life. The poem, in literal translation, is as follows:

曉發草亭日未生	*Leaving the country inn as the morning dawns,* *Before the sun has risen over the valley,*
溪間石路跨驢行	*I ride forth upon my donkey and labor up the stony mountain path.*
秦皇覇業猶留跡	*Yonder in the distance, under the shining sun,* *I see the majestic work of the mighty Emperor of Qín:*
千古依然萬里城	*The thousand mile wall of a thousand years ago;* *Still unchanged, immutable for all eternity.*

先憂後楽

Being the words of a philosopher and saint, the thought couched in the words of this poem is well expressed in an Oriental motto: he was "the first to suffer, the last to enjoy." Thinking how much more my father might have achieved had he lived to a greater age, I might indulge in loud lamentation. I feel, though, that lamentation is needless. His temple, which may appear at first glance to be an anachronism, is animated by his spirit—a vital spirit working for social reconstruction.

Inoue Genichi
Tokyo, Japan
October 31, 1920

I

Inoue Enryo's Guide to the Temple Garden of Philosophy

1. Introductory Remarks

When I resigned from the Philosophy Academy, today's Toyo University, I first thought of the Temple Garden of Philosophy as my retirement place. Yet, due to the subtlety of the precinct and the purity of its ether, it suggested itself naturally as a place for mental cultivation. Therefore, I wanted it to become a park on the outskirts of Tokyo for cultivating students—or young people in general. I enlarged its area and erected more buildings. Beginning in 1906, I dedicated myself exclusively to its management, and finished its basic structures. Thereafter, I established Sunday lectures and summer courses. I also offered a supervised study room that allowed students from all schools in town to stay overnight. I myself am in charge of supervision from morning to evening. Looking at the students in today's society, it is often the case that they have "excellent literary skills, but they lack the ability of judgment" (cf. Analects 5.22). My humble self, for the remainder of my life I want only to care for them and guide the most brilliant talents under heaven. Therefore, when the main hall is finished and the methods of its maintenance are established, I will not pass on the Garden to my descendants. Since my original intention is solely to contribute to the nation, I decided to either transform everything into a foundation, or donate it to the government when the time comes for me to enter eternal sleep. From now on, I will take the task of the Philosophy Shrine as my only joy. I will work as usual, without thinking about myself or the old age to come.

While naming and explaining the 77 Features in the Temple Garden of Philosophy one by one (see Appendix A), I will now guide visitors on a route through the park.

2. Entrance Section

At the entrance to the Garden there are two stone pillars. The right pillar shows the inscription ① Gateway to Philosophy, and the left, ② Realm of Truth. This expresses that, within this precinct, the universal truth of philosophy can be savored, and the magic of life enjoyed.[3] Passing the pillars, there is a building to the right side called the ③ House of Praise, which was erected for monitoring the entrance. To the left side there is the main gate, which is called the ④ Portal of Metaphysics,[4] and which leads to the ⑮ Shrine of the Four Sages. On its posts is written:

[right:]	棹論理舟溯物心之源	*Punting the Boat of Logic upriver to the Source of Mind and Body.*
[left:]	鞭理想馬登絶對之峰	*Whipping the Horse of the Ideal, rising to the Summit of the Absolute.*

Instead of the Humane Kings (Jp. *niō*) as protective deities, inside the pillars of the gate there are sculptures (by TANAKA Yoshio) of a kobold (*tengu*) and a ghost.[5] This

仁王

田中良雄　天狗

3 The inscription on the back side of the right pillar says, "Erected in the Second Year of Great Justice [1913]" 大正二年建立, and on the back of the left, "Shrine Principal Inoue Enryō" 堂主井上圓了. The memorial stone on the left hand side before passing the pillars commemorates the Tokyo municipality's selection of the Temple Garden of Philosophy as a special scenic spot in 1932.

4 Before coming to the gate, there is another memorial stone on the right hand side indicating the Philosophy Shrine 哲學堂. The inscription on the back says, "Start of Construction in the 37th Year of Enlightened Rule [1904] / Founder and Manager Inoue Enryō / Architect and Designer Yamao Shinzaburō" 明治三十七年起工　設立者兼經營者　井上圓了　建築設計技師　山尾新三郎.

5 The tablets on top of the pillars say, on the left, "There is a Ghost inside the Portal of Mystery" 妖怪門幽靈在此内; and on the right, "There is a Kobold inside the Portal of Mystery" 妖怪門天狗在此内.

Figure 2. Portal of Metaphysics

might seem a little bit odd; but, in fact, the ⑫ Kobold Pine and the (70) Ghost Apricot from which this pair derives, are also on these grounds (see chap. 15).

People in society believe that things like kobolds and ghosts are nothing but superstition. Yet, there is a grain of truth in them. Generally, in the world of matter as well as in the world of mind, the principle of the irrational, or, in other words, the incomprehensible, lies at the bottom. Every time someone in the material world comes into contact with the incomprehensible, the image of a kobold arises. When, on the other hand, a similar feeling comes about in the mental world, it takes the shape of a ghost. The kobold is material and, at the same time, equivalent to Yáng. The ghost is spiritual, and equivalent to Yīn. Hence the former is male, and the latter female. This philosophical significance is expressed by the verses,

陽
陰

[right:]	物質精氣凝爲天狗	*When the material ether freezes, a kobold becomes.*
[left:]	心姓妙用發爲幽靈	*When the mind's dynamic engages, a ghost emerges.*

This is why the ④ Portal of Metaphysics is also called the Gate of Mystery.[6]

妖怪門

The fence in line with the Gate separates the realm of the ordinary pluralistic view of philosophy from the realm of the monist view. Therefore, I named it the ⑤ Hedge of Monism. Pluralism is the perspective that distinguishes all things and facts. Monism is rightly understood as a word that points to the one great principle that lies hidden at the bottom of all things and facts. The gate on the other side of the fence serves as the ordinary entrance and exit, for which it is called the ⑥ Gate of Common Sense. The captions on its posts say:

[left:]	四聖堂前月白風清	*Before the Four Sages Shrine, the white moon and the clear wind.*
[right:]	六賢臺上山紫水明	*Above the Pagoda of the Six Wise Men, the purple mountain, the crystal mist.*

3. The Skull Hermitage and the Hollow of Gods and Spirits

Next to the ⑥ Gate of Common Sense, there is a building named the ⑦ Skull Hermitage. Although there is indeed a skull hung up, the name signifies spiritual rather than

6 Because of his fancy for the mysterious, folk beliefs, and all sorts of apparitions, Inoue Enryō was known among his contemporaries as "Doctor Specter" or "Ghost Doc" お化け博士 or 妖怪博士.

physical death.[7] Spiritual death means that a mind that is defiled by the dirt of the secular world vanishes upon entering this hermitage. The skeleton symbolizes the death of the defiled mind and ordinary feelings. I hope that visitors will take a break here and write their names and addresses in the guest book. Some tea will be served. Do not hesitate to ask the gate keeper.

There is a small passage linked to the Skull Hermitage, which is named the ⑧ Corridor of Resurrection. This is an allegory of the defiled mind that has to die so that it can be revived and its philosophical eye newly opened. This is the same as the Zen Buddhist teaching that we first have to kill our mind in order to revive it. From here, the mind leaves the secular world and enters the spiritual realm. The two-storied building which is linked to the Corridor of Resurrection is hence called the ⑨ Hollow of Gods and Spirits. The ground floor is called the ⑩ Chamber to Touch the Divine, and the upper level, the ⑪ Loft of Spiritual Light. Here, distinguished guests can be welcomed when the resting room in the Skull Hermitage becomes too crowded. In the grove of pine trees next to the reception room, there is one tall tree that stands out. It came to be called the ⑫ Kobold Pine, and, seen from far away, it is the signpost of the Philosophy Garden.[8] Somebody even made a verse: "One tree above all, on Peaceful Paddy Hill . . . it's the Kobold Pine!" According to a legend from the village, several times when the pine was about to be cut down, the spook of a kobold prevented the undertaking. It is even said that there was blood pouring out of

和田山や一本高し
天狗松

7 The skull is preserved in the Nakano History Museum 中野区立歴史民俗資料館 (Nakano-kuritsu Rekishi Minzoku Shiryōkan). Tōkyō-to 東京都, Nakano-ku 中野区, Ekoda 江古田 4-3-4.

8 The withered tree was cut down in 1933.

FIGURE 3. Withered Kobold Pine, 1932

the tree. Since the pine is taken to be a kobold, the other hundreds of small pine trees could be called the Needles of the Kobold.

Now, following the exploration route, I will explain the inner garden.

4. The Shrine of the Four Sages

Exiting the ⑦ Skull Hermitage, the first thing to see is the ⑮ Shrine of the Four Sages, which should be regarded as the focal point of the Garden, or as its main hall. The open area around the Shrine represents the philosophical notions of time and space, and is therefore called the ⑬ Hill of Time and Space. The bushes on the side I named the ⑭ Thicket of One Hundred Subjects. The Shrine of the Four Sages is a rectangular building, in the center of which

FIGURE 4. Shrine of the Four Sages

a sculpture is located.[9] But, rather than being an idol of religious worship, this sculpture represents the Ideal of philosophy. Generally, it is matter and mind that are the starting point and the basis—or the eyes and the bones—of philosophy. Agonizing over how to give mind and matter symbolic form, I decided to hang a spherical lantern

9 At the front side of the Shrine, that is, the side facing the ⑬ Hill of Time and Space, there is a memorial stone that was placed there by Toyo University in 1999. The inscription says: "A Park to Cultivate the Mind. Professor Inoue Enryō was born in a temple in New Lagoon 新潟 (Niigata) Prefecture, at a time when Japan's old feudal regime opened the country to the world. After the Enlightened Rule 明治 (Meiji) era had begun, Inoue Enryō studied in the Philosophy Department of Tokyo University's Faculty of Letters. There he felt the necessity for a new mindset that would face the world, the universe, and humanity during this period of sweeping change. With this idea in mind, in 1887 he founded the Philosophy Academy, the origin of today's Toyo University, in order to educate people in creative thinking. Inoue Enryō also visited more than half of all the cities, towns, and villages in the entire country, and tirelessly taught the idea of a good world and a righteous mind. He poured all of the honoraria and donations he received during the immense task of his nationwide lecture tours into the building of this park. Aspiring for public benefit, Professor Inoue Enryō built this place for cultivating the mind of the people, and gave it the name Temple Garden of Philosophy. We record here our wish to commemorate the 80th anniversary of the Professors death. Toyo University"

FIGURE 5. Sculpture of the Absolute

in the center. Because the heart (the original meaning of the pictogram for "mind") appears to be round, red, and translucent, it should hence be light. The lamp takes the shape of a heart for the same reason. Next is matter,

心

物

which stands in direct opposition to mind and therefore should be square, black, and opaque. Since matter is what defiles mind, I ventured to place a censer underneath the lamp. On the framework of the square censer takes the English word and the Sino-Japanese character for "matter" are written. Although our original mind is pure and undefiled, our senses are stimulated by the outer material world. This induction of all sorts of cravings and delusions is expressed by the smoke of the incense that obfuscates the transparency of the spherical lantern. The design suggests that even if our mind sometimes gets defiled by worldly desires, its purity will be conserved through the continuous practice of mental cultivation—just like the original transparency of the lamp can be maintained by sweeping and polishing its clouded surface from time to time.[10]

5. The Ceiling of the Shrine of the Four Sages

Next, I ruminated over the arrangement above mind and matter. Although philosophy starts out from mind and matter, if their original substance is in question, a higher existence necessarily must be supposed. This substance can be named in several ways: the Absolute, the Unlimited, or the Unknowable. This original substance has no form or color, and hence it is something that ultimately cannot be represented. If we, however tentatively, conceptualize the original source of mind and matter from

10 The lantern and the censer were lost due to burglary before 1957. Since 2019, a reproduction of the sculpture hangs under the ceiling instead (see fig. 5). The black lacquer sculpture of the lying Buddha entering *nirvāna*, by the artist Wada Kaheiji 和田嘉平次, was placed in the Shrine in 1940. It is not part of Enryō's original design.

the perspective of form, the vast cosmos—or the dense world itself—may be perceived as the womb of mind and matter at the primordial and chaotic beginning of time. Therefore, I had the idea to represent the condition before the creation of the world. In order to shed light on the primeval times when heaven and earth were not yet separated, a comparison can be made to a chicken's egg. This analogy of the chicken's egg exists in Japan and China.[11] And because there is the idea of emanation from a great egg in India as well, I attached a hemisphere of golden metal in the center of a ceiling made of silver glass. The gold stands for the yolk, the silver for the white of the egg. The former is the divine substance of the universe containing the element of life; the latter is the stuffing of the universe containing life's nourishment. The element of life sublimes to become the mental element, and the nourishment solidifies and forms the element of matter. In order to express this, I decided to arrange the spherical lantern perpendicularly underneath the golden hemisphere, and to suspend the square censer from the frame of the silver glass. The four corners of the ceiling equal the four celestial directions. In the dimension of shape, this design expresses the original substance of mind and matter, that is, the Absolute. It is further possible to correlate heaven, earth, and mankind with the square ceiling, the censer, and the lantern, respectively. Moreover, the round rafters of the ceiling around the installation represent rays of light radiating from the divine substance of the universe. They can be interpreted as the light of the

11 In his book『外道哲學』[Heterodox philosophy] (IS 22: 463–66), Enryō cites Buddhist, Chinese, and Japanese sources to show that the idea of a primordial world egg is common to all three traditions.

Truth, the Good, and the Beautiful emanating from the substance of the Absolute. Since I took mind to be round and matter to be square, I decided that the Shrine's posts had to be round and its base square.

武田吾一
大澤三之助
古宇田實
山尾新三郎

In order to realize the expression of my philosophical ideal in architecture, I conferred with TAKEDA Goichi, ŌSAWA Sannosuke, and KOUDA Minoru. The concrete plans were made by YAMAO Shinzaburō. Having not more than a few pennies, I tried to build while spending minimally. Therefore, I could realize only a small part of my ideal. The gentlemen who will look at the design will certainly laugh at it as being like some kind of child's play. However, my hope is that part of my effort will also be grasped.

6. The Selection of the Four Sages

Having explained the plan of the ⑮ Shrine of the Four Sages, we may now turn our attention to the actual four sages to whom this shrine is dedicated. They are Buddha, Confucius, Socrates, and Kant.

As has been stated above, the principal subjects of philosophy are matter, mind, and the universe. They do not, however, explain man. Rather, it is human beings—the philosophers of all times and places, the ones who see into the hidden meaning of these subjects and reveal their truths—who must explain them. I intended to consecrate this Temple Garden of Philosophy to those seers, but, when I considered their vast number, I decided to select four representative sages from among them.

The philosophy of the present day is divided into two groups: that of the West and that of the East. Oriental philosophy may further be sub-divided into two groups,

Chinese and Indian; and Occidental philosophy may be classified as Ancient and Modern. It was for this reason I decided that one philosopher out of each of these groups should be selected and enshrined.

As we know, Lǎozǐ (Old Master) and Confucius are two great figures in Chinese philosophy. Most Oriental people, however, are drawn to Confucius. In Indian philosophy, on the other hand, Buddha holds the highest place. If we turn to Occidental philosophy, among the ancient philosophers we find such great men as Plato and Aristotle. But the man who founded this philosophical tradition, and who was also the greatest teacher of his time, was Socrates. It is for this reason that I have selected Socrates to represent the philosophy of the Occident.

老子

Modern philosophy has produced a multitude of great advocates, each vying with the other for supremacy. Yet, the German philosopher Kant is the one man among the many who can be chosen as a representative of modern philosophy, for it was he who swayed the entire philosophical world of Europe during his lifetime.

These four great philosophers—Buddha, Confucius, Socrates, and Kant—possess the quintessence of learning and the rarest virtue as to character. They are true representatives of the philosophical world, and I therefore enshrined those four holy sages in this edifice. Four wooden tablets, on which the names of the four philosophers (i.e., "Sage Confucius," "Sage Buddha," "Sage Socrates," and "Sage Kant") are inscribed, are hung aloft, surrounding the design symbolizing heaven and the universe. Graphically, this idea is expressed in figure 6.

孔聖 釋聖
瑣聖 韓聖

There are those who ask why Jesus Christ was not included among those chosen. This Temple Garden, being a garden for philosophy rather than religion, makes

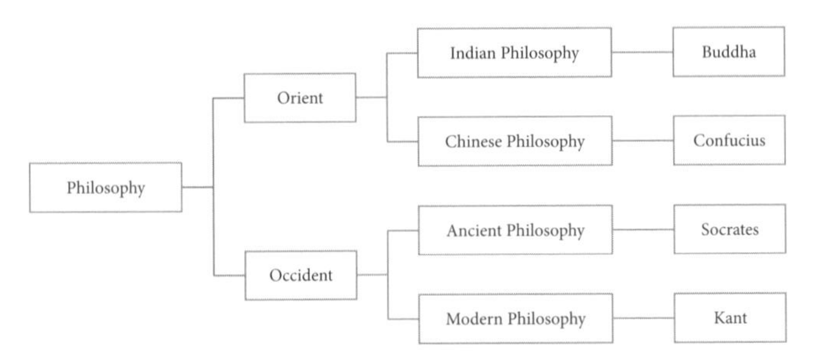

FIGURE 6. Diagram of the Four Sages

the exclusion self-explanatory. Jesus Christ was a world savior, not a philosopher. If we turn to the pages of any history of philosophy, we shall never find therein any mention of Jesus Christ. On the contrary, Buddha is recognized as a world savior—and as a philosopher as well—both in the East and in the West.[12]

FIGURE 7. Mantra Pillar with wooden Heart Drum

7. The Mantra Pillar

During an earlier period, I attempted to bring the ideas of universe, mind, and matter into contrast in the ⑮ Shrine of the Four Sages. At a later period, I introduced quite another idea, that is to say, the idea of invocation. The

12 According to INOUE Enryō's will, a ceremony is to be held every year in commemoration of one of the Four Sages. This Philosophy Ceremony 哲學祭, known today as the Philosophy Shrine Ceremony 哲學堂祭, takes place in the Temple Garden of Philosophy on a Sunday in the first half of November. On these occasions, a Portrait of the Four Sages by WATANABE Bunsaburō 渡邊文三郎 is displayed (cf. Appendix B).

former is nothing but an idealistic symbolism, having an upward tendency, while the latter is a practical idea, with a downward tendency. To symbolize this practical tendency, in the center of the shrine I have placed a small marble stele, which stands on a stone slab. This pillar, called the ⑯ Mantra Pillar, bears the inscription *Namu Zettai-mugen-son.*[13] There is a tablet in the shrine that explains the method of invocation.

南無絶對無限尊

余思ふに哲學の極意は、理論上宇宙眞源の實在を究明し、實際上其本體に我心を結託して、人生に樂天の一道を開かしむるに外ならず。此に其體を名けて絶對無限尊といふ。空間を極めて涯なきを絶對とし、時間を盡して際なきを無限とし、高く時空を超越して、而も威徳廣大無量なるを尊とす。之に我心を結託する捷徑は、只一心に南無絶對無限尊と反復唱念するにあり。

It is my belief that the ultimate object of philosophy is to investigate theoretically the universal source of being, and then to link this truth to the human mind—thus opening a path of optimism in real life. I have called the ultimate object of invocation *Zettai-mugen-son.* The Japanese word zettai signifies endless, universal space, mugen means infinity of time, and son signifies transcendence over time and space as well as immeasurable great virtue and dignity. The quickest way to link our minds with the Absolute Infinite Supreme is to recite repeatedly the sacred formula, "Hail, Absolute Infinite Supreme!"

13 The photograph shows the Mantra Pillar with a wooden percussion instrument in front of it. Similar instruments are used in Buddhist rituals to keep rhythm during recitation. Those drums are called "wooden fishes" 木魚 because of their shape. However, the instrument which is today held by the Nakano History Museum (see note 7) is shaped like the Western heart icon ♡, is red, and has written on it the Chinese pictograph of the human heart 心, which also means "mind."

人一たび之を唱念するときは、忽ち鬱憂は散じ、苦惱は滅し、不平は去り、病患は滅じ、百邪の波はおのづから鎭まり、千妄の雲は自然に收まり、立ろに心海に樂乾坤を開き、性天に歡日月を現じ、方寸場頭に眞善美の妙光を感得するに至る。之と同時に宇宙の眞源より煥發せる偉大なる靈氣が我心底に勃然として湧出するに至る。其功徳實に不可思議なり。而してこれを唱念する方法に三樣あり。

Should this sacred formula be uttered but once, it will banish all melancholy, kill agony, remove discontent, lesson physical pain, and calm the raging sea of evil thoughts. It will disperse the clouds of doubt and illusory fancies; it will bring Heaven to the spirit, and bless one with divinely happy days; it will thus, even on this small spot, bring onto us the mystic light of Truth, Goodness, and Beauty. At the very instant of uttering this sacred formula, the all-powerful universal Spirit gushes forth by mighty emanations, and rouses to life within one. The effect of this mantra is to bring inscrutable marvels to us. There are three different ways of practicing the mantra:

誦唱＝聲を發して南無絶對無限尊を唱ふ。

The vocal mantra: with audible voice, we utter the sacred words, *Namu Zettai-mugen-son.*

默唱＝口を塞ぎて南無絶對無限尊を唱ふ。

The silent mantra: with closed lips, we silently utter the sacred words, *Namu Zettai-mugen-son.*

默念＝目を閉じて南無絶對無限尊を唱ふ。

The concentration mantra: with closed eyes, we meditate in silence on the sacred words, *Namu Zettai-mugen-son.*

此唱念法によりて我心地に安樂城を築き、進じ國家社會のため、獻身的に奮鬪活躍するを哲學堂（自稱道德山哲學寺）に於て唱道する教外別傳の哲學とす。

Through the force of the mantra, we can build up perfect bliss and tranquility within our minds; and we shall be aided in sacrificially and zealously exerting ourselves in the interests of our country and our fellow men as well. This is the unorthodox philosophy transmitted in the Philosophy Temple on Mount Morality.

FIGURE 8. Pagoda of the Six Wise Men

8. THE PAGODA OF THE SIX WISE MEN

After the visitor has completed his inspection of the ⑮ Shrine of the Four Sages, by retracing his steps about fifteen meters he may now see a pagoda. It is three-storied, red, and hexagonal in shape. At the six corners of the slanting roof, molded in the tile, the face of a kobold looks down. Upon entering this structure, one finds that six philosophers have been enshrined on the top floor; hence it is called the ⑰ Pagoda of the Six Wise Men. In contrast to the Four Sages, who are world philosophers, the Six Wise Men are Oriental philosophers. Two each have been chosen from Japan, China, and India. Shōtoku Taishi and Sugawara no Michizane represent Japan; Zhuāngzǐ and Zhū Xī, China; and Nāgārjuna and Kapila, India.

聖徳太子
菅原道眞　莊子
朱熹

Shōtoku Taishi, who introduced Buddhism into Japan, was the father of Japanese civilization. Sugawara no Michizane is regarded as an early father of learning and calligraphy in Japan. Both scholars are venerated as national Gods. In China, Zhuāngzǐ, from the ancient Zhōu dynasty, is glorified in Taoism; and Zhū Xī was the great commentator of Confucianism during the Sòng dynasty.

周

宋

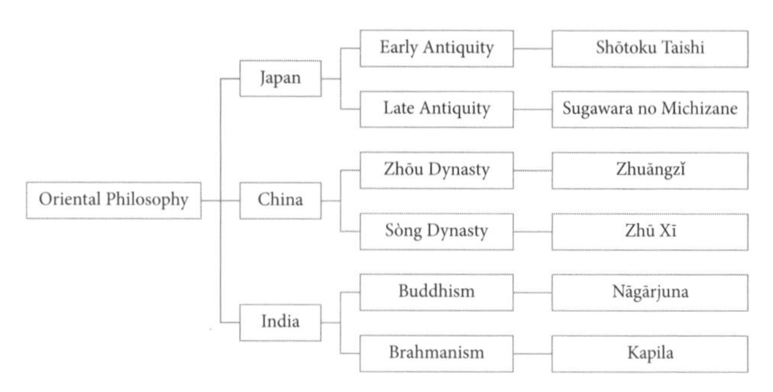

FIGURE 9. Diagram of the Six Wise Men

In India, there once arose a serious dispute between the followers of Buddhism and the Brahmin philosophers. Nāgārjuna rose in defense of Buddhist philosophy and, conquering his opponents, became the leader of Indian thought. He is therefore regarded as a restorer of Buddhism. The Brahmin philosophy was divided into several schools. Among them, the one most highly evolved metaphysically is the Sāṃkhya School. As Kapila was the originator of this philosophy, we have chosen him to represent Brahmin philosophy. Figure 9 indicates their classification.

Portraits of the Six Wise Men hang from the ceiling, encircling a bell which hangs from the center. The name of each wise man is engraved on the bell facing his portrait. If anyone wished to ring this bell, he must ring it six times, two short beats at a time, thus notifying each of the Six Wise Men.[14]

中澤弘光
津田信夫
山尾新三郎

NAKAZAWA Hiromitsu is the painter of the portraits, TSUDA Nobuo is the artist who cast the bell, and YAMAO Shinzaburo is the architect of this building. On

14 The bell was lost due to burglary before 1957. An information board on the upper floor is of later origin. It contains no information beyond what is written in this guide.

the middle floor, stoneware and porcelain that I collected from various places in the course of my many journeys are exhibited. Even common stones picked up in the streets of London, New York, and Paris are on exhibition here. In this collection the visitor may also find maple leaves from the Himalaya Mountains as well as several hundred amulets which I have collected from different shrines and temples since 1891.[15]

9. The Route to the Garden of Materialism

Leaving the ⑯ Pagoda of the Six Wise Men, we walk down the slight slope by the old ⑫ Kobold Pine. Turning to the right here, we find the ⑱ Brush Tomb on the right-hand side of the path. Shaped like a brush, this tomb is a memorial stone to the writing brushes that were used in accumulating the funds for the establishment of the Temple Garden of Philosophy. On the erection of this tomb in 1915, I composed a humorous poem, running thus:

字をかきて耻をかく	*Short is the time that I shall suffer*
のも今暫し哲學堂の	*The humiliation my poor pen brings in its wake;*
出来上るまで	*For soon will the temple be raised aloft*
	And my poor pen freed from its task!

On the front of the memorial stone for my brushes I have inscribed the following words:

15 What has not been lost of Enryō's souvenirs is today preserved in the Nakano History Museum (see note 7).

余欲建設哲學堂使人修養心身荷筆歷遊諸洲應需揮毫積其謝報充此資大半既成於是築筆塚以記其由云

Desiring to build this Temple Garden of Philosophy for the cultivation of body and mind, I have wandered from place to place with my brush in hand. At the request of those who were interested, I have wielded my pen from morning to night. In this manner I have accumulated money for the building fund. Since half the task is done, I now erect on this spot the tomb of the brush.

大正四年一月
井上圓了并書

January, Year Four of Great Justice [1915]
[Text] and Calligraphy by Inoue Enryō

This tomb is also an acknowledgment of the good will of the people who bought my writings and an apology for my bad penmanship.

After we pass the tomb and proceed along the path, we reach a dividing point called the ⑲ Fork of Doubt. If we continue straight on our way, we shall reach the ㉗ Garden of Materialism. If we swerve to the left, we shall reach the ㊼ Garden of Idealism. We are now confronted with a dilemma here. Shall we choose the path that leads to Materialism, or the one that takes us to Idealism? This is the serious conflict that we encounter at the Fork of Doubt.

Philosophy takes us along two paths—one is that of the mental, and the other is that of the material. Each one of us must choose between the two. Following the path of the mind, we shall reach its final goal, which is idealism; and following the path of matter, we shall reach the final goal thereof, which is materialism. It is for this reason that I have laid out two gardens: one, the Garden of Idealism on the western border of the Temple Garden, and the other, the Garden of Materialism on its eastern border.

We could say that experiences are stepping-stones to materialism. Materialism is the result of studies of the empirical sciences, such as physics, chemistry, and biology. The pass that leads to the Garden of Materialism is therefore called the ⑳ Slope of Experience. All of the other terms in this part of the garden are taken from the empirical sciences as well.

At the middle point of the Slope of Experience, we find a small mound called the ㉑ Peak of Perception. This mound signifies that experiences depend upon the senses, such as hearing and seeing. Looking down from this mound, we see a small marshy pool, fan shaped, over the narrow end of which is a bridge (see ㊵ and ㊶ in the next chapter).

If we now turn to the right and walk into the pine forest, which has been named the ㉒ Grove of Endless Beings, we reach a flight of three marble steps. These steps, called the ㉔ Tripartite Podium, are intended as a resting place dedicated to the Three Fathers of Philosophy: the Yellow Emperor of China, Akṣapāda of India, and Thales from Greece. We have erected three stone steles, engraved with likenesses of the three philosophers that are accompanied by short sketches of their lives (see part III, chap. 3). This corner of the park is therefore called the ㉓ Three Founders Yard, and the stone steles are called the ㉕ Monument of the Three Founders.

We find an irregular path running through the Grove of Endless Beings. This path is called the ㉖ History of Philosophy Path. As we stroll along this route, we come across a wooden tablet, on which we read a chronicle of world philosophers.[16]

16 The wooden tablet does not exist anymore.

Figure 10. Matter Patch before Shelter of Objectivity and Telescope Catwalk, 1932

10. The Garden of Materialism

Leaving the ㉓ Three Founders Yard and the monument dedicated to them, we descend by the stone steps to the ㉗ Garden of Materialism. Spreading out in the center of the Garden is a patch in the form of the Chinese character that means "matter." It is the symbol for this part of the garden. Passing the ㉘ Matter Patch, the visitor may rest in a small wooden kiosk, named the ㉙ Shelter of Objectivity.[17] Adjacent to it are the ㉜ Weir of Natural History and the ㉛ Pool of Science.

A river runs through the southern side of the Temple Garden of Philosophy. Where it flows through the scientific spheres of the Garden of Materialism, it is called the

17 Genichi notes that the ㉙ Shelter of Objectivity was destroyed by air raid during the war, along with the (55) Pavilion of Subjectivity. It was rebuilt between 1990 and 1993 (Miura 2002).

FIGURE 11. Mount Fuji Bridge

FIGURE 12. Crescent Moon Balcony before Shelter of Objectivity

㉝ Brook of Mathematics. Two small bridges have been built across this small river. The first, named the ㉟ Telescope Catwalk, was formerly a ropeway with a basket, and therefore also called Ascension Bridge. The second, called the ㉞ Observation Overpass is, architecturally, a suspension bridge that is shaped like Prosperous Lord Mountain

昇天橋

富士淺

Figure 13. Tanuki Lamp

(Mt. Fuji), and hence is also called the Arch of the Prosperous Lord (see figure 11). Crossing the Observation Overpass, we reach the ㊱ Starry Land. Here is the ㊲ Crescent Moon Balcony, which may be used as a music stand.[18]

Now we turn our attention to the hillside. We re-cross the river via the bridge. The ㉚ Furrow of Evolution runs along the base of the hill. Behind the furrow there is a grotto named the ㊳ Grotto of Mysticism. Its dark recess is meant to symbolize the mystery of creation. The furrow has its source here, in the water that drips from the dark walls. Thus also, the theory of Evolution leads back to mysticism, as we follow the theory of materialism to its origin.

扇狀沼

Next we come to the Fan-shaped Marsh, which is called the ㊵ Swamp of the A Posteriori. A Posteriori is a philosophical term meaning "that which first arises through experience." The bridge at the narrower end of the marsh is the ㊶ Bridge of the Atoms, popularly called the Fan-skeleton Bridge. The fan shape symbolizes the atoms, which, through creative power, gradually enlarge and branch out until they evolve into the world of

扇骨橋

18 The ㉟ Telescope Catwalk (see fig. 10) and the ㊲ Crescent Moon Balcony (see fig. 12) are lost. The ㉞ Observation Overpass was rebuilt as modern bridge between 1990 and 1993 (Miura 2002). The Philosophical Garden of the Hungarian artist, Wagner Nándor (1922–1997), was set up in 2009, on the grounds of the ㊱ Starry Land.

civilization. Near the bridge we see a spring. I have called this spring ㊷ Nature's Fountain because its waters gush fourth continuously, symbolizing the constant creative impulse of the Universe.[19]

There is a stone lantern, called ㊴ Tanuki Lamp. It represents one aspect of life. The tanuki is said to be full of deceit and cunning—as is man. Man is deceitful, untruthful, possessed of false pride, given to flattery, and prone to exaggerate. Yet, in the midst of these vices in man, a spiritual light shines forth. To symbolize this truth, a lantern has been placed in the stomach of the tanuki.[20]

11. The Route to the Garden of Idealism

As we bend our way eastward from ㊷ Nature's Fountain, we stroll along the ㉝ Brook of Mathematics toward the ㊼ Garden of Idealism. A few paces later, on the left hand side of the path, is a stone slab bearing the words, ㊸ Ravine of Creation. The Ravine of Creation has been artificially formed out of the hillside. Among the stones and rocks that have been piled up here and there within the hollow, water freely trickles through from a hidden source; this section of the secret spring is also one of the functions of creation.[21]

19 ㊷ Nature's Fountain dried up due to the lowering of the groundwater level with increasing urbanization. It was rebuilt, together with the ㊵ Swamp of the A Posteriori and the ㊶ Bridge of the Atoms, between 1990 and 1993 (Miura 2002). Next to Nature's Fountain is a sculpture of the monk, Jute Bag 布袋 (Hotei). In Japan, he is considered one of the Seven Deities of Good Luck 七福神. It is the same character as the Chinese Laughing Buddha 笑佛.

20 The ㊴ Tanuki Lamp, swept away in frequent floods, today, has a deformed face and has lost its stand. The Japanese animal called *tanuki* can be translated into English as "raccoon-dog." It belongs to the *Canidae* family.

21 The spring has dried up (cf. note 19).

If we continue our stroll from here, we reach the ㊹ Junction of Dualism. Dualism is also a philosophical term, meaning "a theory that explains the world as the manifestation of the principles of matter and mind standing against each other without being reduced to a single source." The Junction of Dualism is situated between the Garden of Idealism and the Garden of Materialism, serving as a junction for matter and mind.

If we ascend the hill from here, we again reach the ⑱ Brush Tomb. A little further up the hill we see a toilet, pointed to by a signpost with the words, "Here is the indispensable place of human existence."[22] If we walk in the direction of the Garden of Idealism, a few steps will take us to the ㊺ Inlet of Learning. This inlet is meant to convey the idea that here, in the pool of learning, we may cleanse ourselves of the impurities of life. And, if the visitor so desires, he may literally perform the necessary ablutions of his travel-stained clothes.[23]

人生必須之處在此

22 The toilet is not in use anymore.

23 Genichi notes: The above explanation was given by Enryō around 1913. The Route to the Garden of Idealism was then covered with a clump of oak and cedar trees, and was gloomy even in the day. He called the brook Crystal Brook 玉川. It was even more pure and clear around 1898 when I was a boy. At the time when my father purchased the lands that included the ㊻ Chasm of Dogmatism [1902], we could easily fish using a line. There, during summer nights, plenty of fireflies, male and female, radiated lights around us. Thus the surroundings in the Warrior Hide Plain 武藏野 (Musashino) were full of rural life and beauty. Later, the brook got worse and dirty; the water of the river with which we once cleansed ourselves of the impurities of life became insufficient even to wash my feet. We should hold on to the fisherman's words in the verse by the ancient Chinese poet Qū Yuán 屈原: "When the water of the Blue Stream [Ch. Cānglàng 滄浪] is clean, I can wash the cord [of my cap]; when the water of the Blue Stream is dirty, I can wash my feet." 滄浪之水清兮, 可以濯我纓, 滄浪之水濁兮, 可以濯我足.

The road leading from the Inlet of Learning to the Garden of Idealism was formed by cutting away part of the hillside. This road is called the ㊻ Chasm of Dogmatism. Dogmatism is a philosophical term for theories that start with assumed and asserted principles. Dogmatism therefore contrasts with empiricism. The school of empiricism is based on observational and experimental science, whereas Dogmatism is an idealistic conception. Empiricism is connected with the material side of life, while dogmatism is related to the intuitive and idealistic. Therefore, the ⑳ Slope of Experience has been placed in the Garden of Materialism, and the Chasm of Dogmatism has been laid out in the Garden of Idealism, which we will encounter as we continue a few steps along our way.

12. The Garden of Idealism

As we enter the ㊼ Garden of Idealism, stretching before us in the middle of it is the ㊽ Heart-shaped Pond. Like the Chinese character for "matter" in the ㉗ Garden of Materialism, this pond is a symbolic representation of the Garden of Idealism. It has the form of the Chinese character that depicts the human "heart." By heart we mean the mind or the spirit. The pond is flanked on the south by the watercourse—at this location called the ㊾ Depths of Ethics—and on the north by the ㊿ Cliff of Psychology. Ethics and psychology thus face each other. This arrangement represents the mind as a monarch, with ethics and psychology as her counselors on either side.

物

心

There is a miniature island, named the ㉛ Isle of Reason. It is placed thus to symbolize the idea that reason, the essence of the spirit, is to be found in the innermost depths of the mind. A stepping-stone connects the Isle

FIGURE 14. Demon Lantern

of Reason with the shore. This stone is called the ⑬ Bridge of Concepts. Concepts are mental functions that link reason to the outside world.

A lantern nearby, called the ⑫ Demon Lantern, is a figurative expression of the human mind. If we consider that the ㊴ Tanuki Lamp in the Garden of Materialism is a view of biological life, then we may say that the Demon Lantern is a view of the mind. In the human heart there are the demons of evil thoughts and lustful desires. Conscience, on the other hand, is the light in the heart that illuminates and guides us. The Demon Lantern shows the figure of a demon bending under the lantern, which he is compelled to hold over his head. Bowed by the agony of remorse, he holds aloft the light of conscience, which triumphs over evil. Let us hope that it will ever be thus in this world that the power of conscience will suppress the demons within us.[24]

On the far side of the pond is a spring called the ⑭ A Priori Spring. There are moments when, in the innermost depths of the soul, we feel something supreme—something sublime within us. In ethics we call this an "a priori imperative." This supreme command transcends education and experience. A comparison between this

24 Genichi notes: The ⑫ Demon Lantern was washed away by a flood a few years ago. Later, during dredging operations, it was picked up from the riverbed downstream and returned. Now it stands at its former place, missing the lantern and leaving only a spoiled visage of the Demon.

categorical imperative being conveyed to the heart, and the spring, whose pure waters flow into the Heart-shaped Pond, led me to call the spring the A Priori Spring.

In the east corner of the garden, on a slight elevation, we find the (55) Pavilion of Subjectivity. This spot is intended as a resting place for those who wish to reach the spiritual realm. It has been erected as a contrast to the ㉙ Shelter of Objectivity, found in the Garden of Materialism. Here the visitor may rest and sit in silent meditation.[25]

13. The Domain of Logic

Even as the investigation of natural science is based on mathematics, so is the study of philosophy based on Logic. We must therefore set aside a definite section for logic in the Temple Garden of Philosophy.

The logical function of the mind is related to cognition, whose elements are awareness, thinking, and inference. Independent of these elements is spontaneous perception, which is called intuition. Cognition and intuition are both functions of consciousness. In order to express the relation between cognition and intuition, two slopes have been laid out between the ㊼ Garden of Idealism and the ⑬ Hill of Time and Space. The slope to the left is short, and inclines in a straight line; the one on the right runs in a zigzag line, and is longer. The straight slope is known

25 Genichi notes: The ㊼ Garden of Idealism was made by the garden architect Kamagata Junkichi [?]. It is seen as the best among his creations. The (55) Pavilion of Subjectivity was destroyed by fire when it was hit by a bomb toward the end of the war, as was the ㉙ Shelter of Objectivity (cf. note 17). The present Pavilion of Subjectivity is furnished with a stone bench and a table, the last bearing ruled lines for playing Gobang 碁盤 (*goban*) or Japanese Chess 將棋 (*shōgi*).

FIGURE 15. Southern view of the Temple Garden of Philosophy, c. 1920

as the (56) Shortcut of Intuition. The longer slope is called the (57) Road of Cognition. Since intuition is not in the category of logic, but cognition is, we have made the (58) Domain of Logic include the Road of Cognition but not the Shortcut of Intuition.

If we take the Road of Cognition starting from the (48) Heart-shaped Pond, along the way we shall see a small, umbrella-shaped pavilion named the (59) Observatory of Deduction. Advancing a few steps, we reach the crest of the hill where we find three stone benches that serve as a resting place. This place is called the (60) Spot of Induction.

Induction draws from particular facts a general law, whereas deduction leads from general laws to particular facts. To express this idea in popular language, I might say that example before proof is induction, and that proof before example is deduction. Consequently, my reason for placing the Observatory of Deduction in seclusion on the slope of the hill is to show that deduction begins with the general truth within us. The Spot of Induction is on

FIGURE 16. Citadel of the Absolute

the crest of the hill, with a wide outlook, because induction embraces wide views of the outside world.

Hence, in visiting the Observatory of Deduction, one may spend a few moments in self-contemplation; and in viewing from the Spot of Induction, the visitor may permit his gaze to wonder far and wide across the stretch of scenery that meets the eye.[26]

14. THE CITADEL OF THE ABSOLUTE

After passing the (58) Domain of Logic and proceeding up the hill, there is a two-legged bench, called the (61) Station of Consciousness placed between the (57) Road of Cognition and the (56) Shortcut of Intuition. It is appropriate to take a break here and reflect on various things. The hill symbolizes the universe. I called it the ⑬ Hill of Time and Space, as explained before. Time, space, and the universe become the Absolute when bound together. When everything is in opposition to each other, it is called the relative. Arriving at the point where there are no opposites is

26 Today, trees obstruct the view from the (60) Spot of Induction.

called the Absolute—and is the ultimate in philosophy. For example, as matter is opposite to mind, and mind is opposite to matter, they both are relative. If the original source and substance of both mind and matter is pursued, there is no matter and no mind, and one arrives at the point where no naming is possible anymore. This, then, can only be called the Absolute. This is why it was necessary to establish a realm of the Absolute in the precinct of the Philosophy Garden. The building between the ⑥⓪ Spot of Induction and the ⑮ Shrine of the Four Sages is the Reading Hall. Being a representation of the Absolute, I decided to give it the name ⑥② Citadel of the Absolute. If one synthesizes the universe itself, this comes down to the Absolute. The logic of the intertwined thicket of the myriad phenomena is analogue to the countless books that are assembled in the Citadel of the Absolute. To investigate the myriad phenomena evokes the substance of the Absolute. This is the logic of perfecting the wondrous realm of the Absolute by reading countless books. In other words, the books here are taken to be equivalent to the myriad phenomena of the philosophical world.

讀書堂

I collected these books for over thirty years, starting in 1886. Among the Japanese, Chinese, and Buddhist writings which I bought—spending all of my money—there are several dozen thousand writings from before the Enlightened Rule Restoration (*Meiji ishin*). I want to make them available to the public.[27] Japanese and Chinese books are on the right hand side of the Reading Hall, and Buddhist writings are on the left hand side. The ⑥③

明治維新

27 The books are preserved in the library of Toyo University, and are indexed in『哲學堂圖書館圖書目錄』[Catalog of the Philosophy Shrine Library], pub. by Tōyō Daigaku Fuzoku Toshokan 東洋大学付属図書館, [1916] 1985. See Bodiford 2014.

Monument of the Sages is placed at the back wall. Instead of placing sculptures inside the Shrine of the Four Sages, portraits have been engraved here. I provided the following unskilled words as caption.

四聖像記	Inscription to the Portraits of the Four Sages
凡哲學東西相分在東洋支那哲學以孔聖爲宗印度哲學以釋聖爲首西洋則古代以瑣聖爲宗近世以韓聖爲首	Philosophy is generally divided into Eastern and Western philosophy. In the East, there is Chinese philosophy, which takes the sage Confucius as its authority, and Indian philosophy, which takes Buddha as its head. In the West, Socrates is the authority of ancient philosophy; modern times take Kant to be its head.
故本堂欲合祀斯四聖而代表古今東西之諸哲茲刻影像以致讃仰之誠如其位次則從年代前後非有所軒輊也	Therefore, I wish these Four Sages—who represent all philosophers of East and West, ancient and modern—to be revered in the Main Hall. The portraits engraved here deserve sincere praise. Their arrangement follows the order of generation, but there is no hierarchy among them.
大正四年一月 後學井上圓了識并書	January, Year Four of Great Justice [1915] Record and Calligraphy by the Epigone Inoue Enryō

The portraits were engraved by Tanaka Hyakurei, based on sketches by Hashimoto Gahō. Based on what I said above, the repository of books could also be called Cloister of the Sages. A reading room, which I want to be called the (64) Gallery of Ideas, is provided on the upper floor. This interpretation indicates that all sorts of ideas can be refined through reading books. There is also an observation platform on the top of the reading room, which serves as resting place for times when one is tired from reading. I gave it the name (65) Realm of Contemplation,

田中百嶺
橋本雅邦
聖哲院

FIGURE 17. View from the library's Synopsis Platform, c. 1920

大觀臺

or Synopsis Platform, because on this platform it is possible to look afar in all four directions.[28] It allows one to unleash speculation after concentrating on one's imagination for a long time while sitting in the Gallery of Ideas.

大正

This library was opened on the day of the enthronement ceremony of Emperor Great Justice (Taishō) in November, 1915. I placed an ⑥⑥ Enthronement Memorial Stone in front of the library in order to commemorate this for a long time to come.[29] Its inscription says,

28 The ⑥⑤ Realm of Contemplation was rebuilt in 2018.

29 In the entranceway of the library, there is a calligraphy on the left hand side saying, "Memorial Library of the August Great [Enthronement] Ceremony" 御大典記念圖書館.

哲學堂圖書館記

Record of the Library in the Temple Garden of Philosophy

大正四年十一月國家舉大典靡地弗表其慶哲學堂圖書館亦成基于茲矣初甫水井上博士欲設游息之園相攸于和田山攬其形勝嘆曰此不足以養心身乎乃築堂於中央以祀孔子釋迦瑣克剌底韓圖曰四聖堂祀聖德太子菅公莊子朱子龍樹大士迦比羅仙曰六賢臺祀平田篤胤林羅山釋凝然曰三學亭篤胤取於神道羅山取於儒道凝然取於佛道也命其庭曰唯心其園曰唯物統而名焉曰哲學之堂至是圖書館巋然告成所藏和漢舊籍凡六千七百九十二種四萬一千五百八十五卷二萬一千一百九十三册可謂盛矣

In November of the fourth year of Great Justice [1915], the State held the Great [Enthronement] Ceremony. Everywhere [the people] expressed their joy. The Library of the Temple Garden of Philosophy was also founded hereupon. In the beginning, Doctor Hosui Inoue wished to build a pleasure garden. Upon deciding for Peaceful Paddy Hill and gazing upon its magnificent contours, he exclaimed: May not here be both mind and body nourished? Then, he erected a shrine in the center for venerating Confucius, Buddha, Socrates, and Kant, and named it the Shrine of the Four Sages. [To the building for] venerating Shōtoku Taishi, Sugawara no Michizane, Zhuāngzǐ, Zhū Xī, Nāgārjuna, and Kapila, he gave the name Pagoda of the Six Wise Men. [The construction for] venerating Hirata Atsutane, Hayashi Razan, and Shaku Gyōnen, he named the Three Erudites Arbor. He selected Atsutane for the Path of the Gods [Shinto], Razan for the Path of the Literati [Confucianism], and Gyōnen for the Path of Buddha. To one yard he gave the name of idealism, to the other yard the name of materialism. The whole [park] he called the Temple Garden of Philosophy. Thereafter, he announced the establishment of a grand library containing old Japanese and Chinese writings. Altogether, 6792 books, 41585 volumes, and 1193 fascicles may indeed be called a copious amount.

夫道無古今之變教有東西之異博士志在合東西文明以擴充斯道於宇内萬里壯遊既極東西兩洋足跡殆遍坤輿到今猶跋涉海内風餐露宿以導斯民不敢寧處而標其神者哲學堂是也故予併記之俾入斯館者有所觀感興起焉	The Path does not change between past and present, [but] the teachings differ between East and West. It was the Doctor's ambition to unite Eastern and Western civilization. In order to spread this Path under the whole sky, he traveled extensively—thousands of miles—to the farthest reaches of the east and the west. His footprints span almost the entire world. Until this day he travels over land and water, eats in the wind, sleeps in the damp—all in order to unceasingly teach his countrymen. And the symbol of this spirit is the Temple Garden of Philosophy. Therefore, I composed the lines on this stone. May everyone who enters this building experience awe and excitement upon its view.
大正五年歳在丙十一月上瀚	Year Five of Great Justice [1916], Year of the Fire-Dragon, Early November
勺水日下寬譔 藤光雲書 田中良雄鐫	Composed by Shakusui Kusaka Hiroshi Calligraphy by Fuji Kōun Engraved by Tanaka Yoshio

15. Rear Gate

Earlier, I referred to the Cloister of the Sages, the (64) Gallery of Ideas, and the (65) Realm of Contemplation together as the (62) Citadel of the Absolute. As its antipode, I named the dry brook next to the library the (67) Trench of the Relative. The stone bridge that stretches over the trench is the (68) Bridge of the Ideal. And for the small gate beyond the bridge, I chose the name (69) Gate of the Transrational.

There are gateways to the Philosophy Garden at three locations. The ④ Portal of Metaphysics in the front is what normally would be called the main gate. The ⑥ Gate of Common Sense is the ordinary entrance. And the Gate of the Transrational is equivalent to a rear gate. The reason why I named it transrational is because it should be understood that, if philosophical investigation is exerted to the ultimate, a logic of the non-logical is necessarily part of the universe. If the upper wing of this gate is unfastened, it hinges down to the outside; and if the lower wing is uplifted and supported from the inside, a roof is quickly formed. This shows what makes the transrational indeed transrational![30]

Next, there is a thin apricot tree on the left side of the Bridge of the Ideal. The reason why I named it ⑰ Ghost Apricot is because, in the beginning, when I was still living in Horsepaddock (Komagome), I was agitated one night by a ghost appearing under the tree. Looking into things closely, I realized that rays emitted from a lamp inside the house had produced reflections in the branches. I laughed, saying, "The true nature of the ghost is a lamp!" Thereafter, I called the apricot tree the Ghost Apricot. Since there is the ⑫ Kobold Pine in the Philosophy Garden, and taking the two as being husband and wife, I moved the apricot tree here.[31]

駒込

On another occasion, at eleven o'clock in the night, when I opened the door and looked into the garden I saw a light flaring and waning quietly under the apricot tree. Thinking that this is what people call "ghost light," I went closer to have a look. During the daytime the groundskeeper had made a hole in the ground in order to burn raked leaves in it. He had covered it with earth, but the

30 The Gate does not exist anymore, and it is somewhat difficult to imagine. Enryō seems to suggest the metamorphosis of the gate into a roof as an instance of mystery.

31 The tree died around 1941.

FIGURE 18. Universe Hall

fire had continued to burn into the night. So there were apparitions under this tree on two occasions! The design of the ④ Portal of Metaphysics, with the kobold and the ghost on both sides, was inspired by the high pine and this very apricot.

16. THE UNIVERSE HALL AND THE IMPERIAL FORUM

The building next to the (70) Ghost Apricot is the (71) Universe Hall. The separated space inside is the (72) Imperial Forum. I felt the need to set up a Universe Hall because philosophy is a field that researches the universal truth. The Hall is a lecture hall that was built for occasional philosophical lectures, or for holding courses. Philosophy is also a field that examines the principles of society and the State. Hence there was also the need to set up a forum for the most beautiful empire among all countries in the world. So I decided to set up a particular space inside the Universe Hall for the Imperial Rescript on Education to be displayed on a podium. To indicate this concept, there is a writing stretching over both of the Hall's front posts:

教育ニ關スル勅語

[right:]	世界萬邦中 皇國爲最美	*Among all countries in the world,* *this Empire is the most beautiful.*
[left:]	宇宙萬類中 人類爲最尊	*Among all species in the cosmos,* *mankind is the most venerable.*

Accordingly, the Imperial Forum can also be called the Rescript Veneration Room. The interior structure—which has a separate space rotated by forty-five degrees within a square room—I believe to be unique. The plan was made by YAMAO Shinzaburō, based on my idea.[32] Another unique feature is the court headgear shaped tile on the top of the roof, which indicates the existence of the Imperial Forum.

勅語崇拝室

山尾新三郎

To the left side of the Universe Hall there is a small hill in the shape of a triangle—the Triangular Hill. At the top of it there is a small triangle shaped arbor, which is called the ⑬ Three Erudites Arbor.

三角山

17. The Three Erudites Arbor and the Inexhaustible Treasury

The ⑮ Shrine of the Four Sages is global, the ⑰ Pagoda of the Six Wise Men is Oriental; now there was the need to set up something Japanese. Therefore, I devised the ⑬ Three Erudites Arbor. Since in Japanese, "three scholars" (*sangaku*) is phonetically similar to "triangle" (*sankaku*), I employed a design in which everything is made of triangles.

Explaining first the significance of the three scholars, there are three "paths" of learning that have been equally

道

32 The black lacquer sculpture of Shōtoku Taishi 聖徳太子, by the artist WADA Kaheiji 和田嘉平次, was placed in the Imperial Forum in 1940. It is not part of Enryō's original design.

pursued in Japan: Shintoism, Confucianism, and Buddhism. Great scholars of broad learning have arisen from all three traditions. If one were to select one representative of each tradition from among these great scholars, there certainly would be ten different opinions among ten different persons. As for me, I place emphasis on the aspect of broad learning, and therefore selected those figures from the three traditions that have bequeathed the most writings. Upon consulting biographies, I found HIRATA Atsutane for Shintoism, HAYASHI Razan for Confucianism, and Gyōnen for Buddhism, and I decided to honor them here. The engravings on the stone plates that hang from the ceiling of the Three Scholars Pavilion are also a work by TANAKA Yoshio.

平田篤胤　林羅山
凝然

田中良雄

Descending from the Triangle Hill, on the left hand side there is a stone pillar with the inscription, "tail without hair, a fountain not white." These words hint to a place for urinating. If you take out the element "hair" from the character for "tail," and delete the element "white" from the character which means "fountain," the elements *shi* and *sui* are left. If you put these two together, you get the character for "urine."[33] In the back, there stands the ⑭ Inkstone Tomb which forms a pair with the ⑱ Brush Tomb and bears the following inscriptions.

尾無毛泉不白

毛
尾　白
泉　尸
水
尿

33 Besides the graphical, there is obviously also a semantic solution of the riddle.

硯塚	Inkstone Tomb
園中既有筆塚矣 硯豈可無塚哉喩 諸人筆爲男則硯 爲女筆爲夫則硯 爲婦二者相依而 産字育文哲學堂 亦頼此而成予乃 爲之媒妁耳於是 築硯塚云	There is already a tomb for brushes in the garden. How could there be none for the inkstone? Using a human analogy: if the brush is a man, the inkstone is a woman. If the brush is the husband, the inkstone is the wife. The two depend on each other; they give birth to letters and nurture literature. The Temple Garden of Philosophy also took its shape relying on them. Thus I arrange their marriage and erect this Inkstone Tomb hereupon.
哲學堂主　井上圓了記	Recorded by Inoue Enryō, Principal of the Temple Garden of Philosophy
大正七年三月建立	Erected in March, Year Seven of Great Justice [1918]

哲學正氣歌	Poem about the Genuine Spirit of Philosophy
宇宙靈妙氣 浩々塞幽明	*The wondrous ether of the cosmic soul boundlessly pervades darkness and light:*
玄冥而有色	*Obscurity has form;*
寂靜而有聲	*stillness has a voice;*
日星因之現	*The sun emerges from it;*
國土依之成	*the nation depends on it.*
濁爲山川質	*Dullness turns into the texture of mountains and rivers;*
清爲草木生	*purity turns into the life of weeds and trees.*
々中帶神機	*Life bears divine functions within,*
分成禽獸情	*splitting into the sensation of animals;*
々中含靈性	*Sensation comprises spiritual nature,*
凝成人心精	*congealing into the energy of the human mind.*

天地元一體 *Heaven and earth are originally of one substance;*
萬物亦同根 *and so are the myriad things from the same root.*
動植已無別 *Animals and plants are not separate,*
人獸豈異源 *how could human and animals be of different origin?*
親子日與地 *Parent and child are like sun and earth;*
兄弟人與猿 *brothers old and young like humans and apes.*
物心相照應 *Because matter and mind illuminate each other,*
故心見乾坤 *the mind perceives the universe.*
天人相感合 *Because heaven and men accord to each other,*
故天動生魂 *heaven moves the spirit of life.*
宇內萬類在 *Among the myriad species that under the sky exist,*
人實爲最尊 *man is truly the most dignified.*

其心大難窺 *The greatness of his mind is difficult to scrutinize;*
其智深難測 *the depth of his wisdom difficult to measure.*
雖住方寸中 *Even though inhabiting the smallest space,*
照及六合極 *his illumination reaches the ultimate in all directions:*
或入極微際 *Entering the dimension of the subtlest;*
或進絶對域 *or proceeding to the realm of the Absolute;*
貫古今上下 *Connecting ancient and modern, high and low;*
包東西南北 *embracing east and west, south and north.*
明則幽界顯 *If bright, the dark worlds become enlightened;*
暗則白日黑 *if dark, the white sun becomes black:*
欲究其玄妙 *Aspiring to penetrate such mysteries*
是爲哲學職 *is indeed the mission of philosophy.*

哲海開航路 *Discovering routes on the ocean of philosophy,*
三千星霜移 *and navigating three thousand winters.*
希臘震古代 *The Greeks swayed antiquity; the Germans and the*
獨英鳴近時 *English resonate in modern times.*
經驗與獨斷 *Empiricism and dogmatism combat for glory on the*
論壇競雄雌 *stage of debate;*
唯心與唯物 *Idealism and materialism fight for primacy in the aca-*
學林爭本支 *demic grove.*
爛如春花亂 *Inflammation like the stirring of spring blossoms;*
鬱如夏雲滋 *suffocation like the heaping of summer clouds.*
眞理岸猶遠 *The shore of truth is still far;*
何日決大疑 *when will the great doubt be resolved?*

在漢老莊學 *In China, Taoist studies explain heaven;*
與儒俱説天 *Confucianism does the same.*
在竺數勝論 *In India, numerous excellent theories discuss the enig-*
與佛同談玄 *matic, Buddhism does so as well.*
甲論而乙駁 *The first argues, the second objects;*
疑團猶依然 *doubt lingers as before.*
茫々哲學海 *On the vast ocean of philosophy,*
去來途萬千 *coming and going on innumerable routes.*
迷雲杳難認 *The cloud of delusion being somber,*
彼岸在何邊 *the other shore is difficult to realize.*
歸來窺自已 *Taking refuge in self-reflection,*
心天性月懸 *the moon of mind's heavenly nature stands high.*

清影入虚窓 *Lucid reflections pierce the window of emptiness;*
靈光照空谷 *spiritual beams illuminate the valley of nothingness.*
時有浮雲遮 *When hanging clouds impede,*
風拂忽亦復 *the wind soon blows them away again.*
塵隙開浄土 *A filthy fissure reveals the pure land;*
毛孔藏天祿 *pores hoard the heavenly reward.*
死生知有定 *Knowing that birth and death have been decided,*
榮辱何須逐 *why bother about honor and shame?*
披此無字書 *Opening this book without letters;*
清夜傾心讀 *reading devotedly in the clear night.*
理性放幽香 *When reason unbinds its esoteric odor,*
滿身自馥郁 *the body's full fragrance naturally abounds.*

井上圓了撰并書 Composition and Calligraphy by Inoue Enryō

Next, there is another of my unskilled verses placed on the backside of the ④ Portal of Metaphysics. Expressing the idea of philosophy, the twelve Sino-Japanese characters say:

FIGURE 19. Inexhaustible Treasury

[right:]	一心大海起 智情意之波	*The Great Ocean — the One Mind raises* *the waves of Wisdom, Emotion, and Will.*
[left:]	絶對古月放 眞善美之光	*The Old Moon — the Absolute radiates* *beams of Truth, Goodness, and Beauty.*

It is my wish that people unable to understand the meaning of these words may enter the Garden and try to savor philosophy themselves.

Continuing the walk from here, we see a detached storehouse. This building is the ㉟ Inexhaustible Treasury, which is the exhibition room. Its upper lever is called ㊱ Edifice of Elevation, and the ground floor is the ㊲ Storehouse of Myriad Phenomena. The building is for the display of the souvenirs I collected during my travels, both domestic and abroad. Apart from the pottery and stoneware (which are on the upper floor of the ⑰ Pagoda of the Six Wise Men), there is a mix of all kinds of things arranged next to each other. There is a shelf for monster sculptures, a shelf for curiosities, and so on. Notably, a wooden statue of the Bodhisattva Mañjuśrī (Jp. Monju; a present from KATSU Kaishū), a picture scroll of the Luminous King Acala, and a carving of the Great King Yama

文殊
勝海舟

are on display. They are the treasures in the compounds of the Temple Garden of Philosophy.[34]

34 What has not been stolen or lost of Enryō's collection is today preserved in the Nakano History Museum (see note 7).

II

Introducing the World Sages

1. The Four Sages of World Philosophy

Name	Inscription	Reading	Meaning
Buddha	釋聖	*Shaka-sei*	Sage Śākyamuni
Confucius	孔聖	*Kō-sei*	Sage Confucius
Socrates	瑣聖	*So[kuratesu]-sei*	Sage Socrates
Kant	韓聖	*Kan[to]-sei*	Sage Kant

Buddha

Śākyamuni Buddha was born in the kingdom of Kapilavastu, in Central India. It is not possible to fix the exact date of his birth because the numerous legends concerning it differ. However, most present-day researchers agree upon April 8, 564 BCE.[35]

Buddha, who was known as Prince Siddhārtha, belonged to the *kṣatriya*, or "warrior" caste. Early in life he displayed a pessimistic tendency, and held no interest in worldly matters. It was his wish to probe the meaning of birth, aging, illness, and death. It is said that, when he was twenty-nine years of age, he took advantage of the courtier's heavy sleep in the dead of night, stealthily rode forth from the palace, and, as a mendicant priest, made his way to Magadha, the center of the civilization of those times. There he visited eminent Brahmin philosophers, but he failed in his aim of finding a teacher. He then

35 This has changed to the contemporary situation, with which many scholars agree, that he must have died around 400 BCE, and thus born around 480 BCE.

abandoned that place and sought enlightenment in the jungle, near the river Nairañjanā, where he spent several years of his life in meditation, practically abstaining from all food and sleep. Finding that these bodily tortures only exhausted him and proved fruitless for the attainment of his goal, he cleansed himself in the river and restored his physical strength with rice and milk.

After that he went to Gayā, where he seated himself on a stone under a Bodhi tree and firmly resolved, even at the cost of his life, not to leave that place before he had attained the state of *saṃbodhi*, true enlightenment. Finally, enlightenment came to him when the Morning Star twinkled in the eastern sky. It is said that this occurred in the early dawn of February, when he was thirty-five. It was there that he gained the perfect knowledge that all agonies connected with birth, aging, illness, and death have their root in ignorance of the true aspect of the universe. This ignorance brings about desires of all kinds, which cause *karma*, or the dynamic chain of good and evil acts. It accumulates and becomes an undercurrent that results in suffering. By banishing this ignorance, thereby eliminating desire and creating no further *karma*, and by seeing the true aspect of life as a selfless being, one shall reach *nirvāṇa*—the ever-peaceful and eternally happy sphere which transcends all earthly agony. Thus did a mendicant priest become the Buddha, the embodiment of truth.

Buddha then left his resting place, crossed the river Ganges, and reached Sārnāth. In this spot he expounded the first sermon, and he continued his teaching for forty-five years, traveling from place to place.

When the time approached for Buddha to die, at the age of eighty, he betook himself to Kuśīnagar Castle. The full moon was shining upon the velvet silence of the night as he sought out a resting place between two Śāla trees. He placed himself between these two trees and addressed himself to his followers assembled there, requesting them to ask him a last question before he should depart this life. His disciples then besought him not to die. To this entreaty he could not yield. Facing his disciples, he expounded his last teaching in the silence of the night. Upon finishing the sermon, he died and passed into the great *nirvāṇa*—resting on his right side, his head to the north, his face to the west—on February 15, 485 BCE, at the age of eighty.

Among the thousands of his followers, Śāriputra, Maudgalyāyana, Ānanda, and Mahākāśyapa are the principal disciples, and of these, Mahākāśyapa is said to have been a major contributor to the compilation of his teachings.

Subsequent to his time, the Buddha's teachings—original Buddhism—developed into Hīnayāna Buddhism, which is somewhat of a natural science or an empirical philosophy. Mahāyāna Buddhism arose at a later time, in revolt against Hīnayāna, and, further developing Buddha's ideas, completed its own metaphysical and religious phase. This theological development came after the Buddha's death. As the Buddha himself had stressed practice rather than theory, original Buddhism was neither Hīnayāna nor Mahāyāna; it embodied principles, however, that could develop into either.[36]

36 Since the Sanskrit *hīna-yāna* (inferior vehicle) has a pejorative meaning, modern scholars use the term Theravāda Buddhism.

Further Reading. Both the *Internet Encyclopedia of Philosophy* (iep.utm.edu) and the *Stanford Encyclopedia of Philosophy* (plato.stanford.edu) have valuable articles on the Buddha, including bibliographies. The article in the latter is, however, rather technical, and it evades the contentious question as to how certain we can be about our knowledge of the historical Buddha. Different from Socrates and Confucius, the teachings of the Buddha were transmitted orally for at least the first three hundred years after his death. Philologically-spirited Buddhist scholars are therefore extremely careful in making further claims about what the Buddha actually taught. Rupert Gethin, who falls into this category, has written the best introduction to Buddhism I am aware of, *The Foundations of Buddhism* (Oxford UP, 1998). For the reader who is open to a hermeneutically fleshed out account of the Buddha's ideas, the book by Richard F. Gombrich, *What the Buddha Thought* (London: Equinox, 2009), is warmly recommended. The translated two-volume work by the Japanese scholar Nakamura Hajime, *Gotama Buddha: A Biography Based on the Most Reliable Texts* (Tokyo: Kosei, 2000/05), should also be mentioned. The *Sutta Nipāta*, which Nakamura considers as one of the most reliable sources regarding the historical Buddha, is moreover a good starting point for one to read the Pali Canon. A shorter option would be the "Discourse on the Setting in Motion of the Wheel" (*Dhammacakkappavattana Sutta*, SN 56.11), which tradition considers as the Buddha's first teaching. Or, one may browse the immensely popular selection of short verses known as the *Dhammapāda*. Translations of the suggested texts, and many more, can be found online on the platform Access to Insight (accesstoinsight.org).

Confucius

孔
魯

Confucius, who is called Kǒng in Chinese, was born in the year 580 BCE, in a small village in the state of Lǔ. Even as a boy when playing with other children, he was meticulous both as to dress and conduct.

Upon reaching maturity, he held several minor public positions. After some time, he left Lǔ in search of still another position. He vainly sought employment in various countries. He returned to Lǔ, but there he was only poorly welcomed. Later, he withdrew from public service to devote himself to studies of poetry, music, and problems of ethics and manners.

詩 樂
禮

Students came to him from near and far. To these he taught about real virtue—the very core of the Confucian doctrine which is contained in the *Analects*. Later on, he toured China with his disciples—frequently at the risk of his own life. His disciples were often filled with fear, but Confucius himself was dauntless. He said, "Heaven gave me virtue, and naught else can stop my course" (cf. Analects 7.23).

論語

In his later years, Confucius became particularly devoted to the study of the *Yìjīng*, or the "Book of Changes," which contains the ancient Chinese philosophy of cosmogony. The leather thongs that tied the tablets of Confucius's copies together were thrice worn out by his constant handling.

易經

He taught his disciples about historical chronology, classical poetry, rites and ancient ceremonies, and the constitution of ancient ideal states as well. He had three thousand disciples, seventy-three of whom were advanced scholars in several sciences—which is marvelous in itself. Yán-yuān has said of Confucius, "Looking up

書
詩 禮
顏淵

at him, we find that he becomes loftier as times goes on, and his character grows firmer and firmer" (cf. Analects 9.11). Mencius says, "There is no character equal to his since the birth of humanity" (cf. Mencius 2B.2).

On certain occasions when touring the country to spread education within the population, he found that his attempts were fruitless. But, in spite of his failures, he did not give way to lamentation, nor did he reproach humanity. On the contrary, he devoted himself more studiously to his own development, saying, "it is only Heaven that knows me" (Analects 14.35). And in his last years he compiled *Chūnqiū*, or the "Spring and Autumn [Annals]," in order to expand the sovereign's power by condemning impiety and disloyalty. He said, "He who values Confucius values the *Spring and Autumn Annals*, he who condemns Confucius condemns the *Spring and Autumn Annals*" (cf. Mencius 3B.13).

春秋

Confucius died at the age of eighty-three, in the year 479 BCE.

Further Reading. The *Encyclopedia of Chinese Philosophy* (ed. A. S. Cua, Routledge, 2003) is a recommended research tool regarding all aspects of Confucian thought. Online, the *Stanford Encyclopedia of Philosophy* (plato.stanford.edu) or the *Internet Encyclopedia of Philosophy* (iep.utm.edu) may be consulted for basic information about Confucius. However, there is no reason not to start reading the *Analects* on one's own. The *Confucian Analects* is by all means the most important text of the Confucian tradition, and it exists in various translations. The classical translation from 1861, by James Legge, is included as digital text in the Chinese Text Project (ctext.

org), and as scan in the Internet Archive (archive.org).[37] The translation by Edward SLINGERLAND, *Confucius Analects* (Indianapolis: Hackett, 2003), is recommended not only because it comes "with selections from traditional commentaries," but also due to its helpful internal cross references. The study by Bruce E. and Takeo A. BROOKS, *The Original Analects: Sayings of Confucius and His Successors* (Columbia UP, 1998), attempts to identify different layers of the texts and reconstruct their chronological order. Hereby touched, the historical truth about the man Confucius and his teachings will continue to be a research subject, as recent archeological findings have led to a reconsideration of the authenticity of another text, the *Sayings of the Confucian School* of which there exists a partial English translation by Robert P. KRAMERS, *K'ung Tzu Chia Yü* (Leiden: Brill Archive, 1950).

孔子家語

Socrates

Socrates, the Sage of Greece, was born in Athens, Greece, in 469 BCE. He was the son of humble parents; his father being a sculptor, and his mother a midwife. He received an ordinary education during his childhood, and he later took up the occupation of his father. As a young man he served in the army, where his enduring valor roused the admiration of all who knew him. In his home life, he displayed maturing patience and kindness towards his wife, who was short-tempered and inclined to laziness.

37 The translation from 1861, published as volume one of James LEGGE's *Chinese Classics* series (Hong Kong), was reprinted "with few alterations" (Preface, 1892) in the revised edition of 1893 (Oxford: Clarendon Press).

Upon reaching more mature years, Socrates became inspired with the ideal of educating young men. It was his custom to seek out such places as public markets, factories, and parks where the common people were wont to assemble. Here, he would engage in conversation with all sorts of men and women—old and young, rich and poor alike—discussing various topics. He exemplified in his own conduct the virtues he taught. Socrates, who had an ugly face, possessed such beauty of heart that all who heard him thought only of his charm and were filled with admiration and reverence.

Sophistry was prevalent in Greece at that time. The people indulged in argument for its own sake rather than in a search for truth. Socrates, thinking that this habit would undermine the morality of the state, strove against it. In striving to correct the evil habits and customs of the time, he aroused the fury of the people and was condemned to death. Although innocent of the charges brought against him, he made no attempt to flee his penalty. Calm and undaunted, he drank a cup of poison and died in 399 BCE, at the age of seventy.

His teaching was that knowledge itself is virtue. He even held that it is impossible to commit evil acts knowingly, and that it is better to suffer from an evil act than to commit it by oneself.

In later years in the Western world, every teacher of education and ethics acknowledged Socrates as the source of his teaching. That so many talented scholars have come from the ranks of his followers—Plato being the most eminent among them—is evidence of this great influence.

FURTHER READING. The Socrates that became influential in Western tradition is the Socrates we know from the

Platonic dialogues. However, both the *Stanford Encyclopedia of Philosophy* (plato.stanford.edu) and the *Internet Encyclopedia of Philosophy* (iep.utm.edu) inform readers about other historical sources and point them to further literature. Recent research regarding the problem of the "real" Socrates is collected in the *Cambridge Companion to Socrates*, ed. by Donald R. MORRISON (Cambridge UP, 2011). The *Apology*, Plato's record of Socrates' defense in court, is not only agreed upon as one of the textual sources close to the historical Socrates, but is also one of the founding documents of Western philosophy and therefore unconditionally recommended for reading. A translation by Harold N. FOWLER (orig. Harvard UP, 1914) is freely accessible in the Perseus Digital Library (perseus.tufts.edu). Other early Platonic texts that have shaped our image of Socrates, for example the dialogues *Laches*, *Charmides*, or *Protagoras*, translated by W. R. M. LAMB (orig. Harvard UP, 1914–1930), can be found in the same database. More recent translations, edited by John M. COOPER et al., are in *Plato: Complete Works* (Indianapolis: Hackett, 1997).

Kant

Immanuel KANT, unrivaled among philosophers, was born in 1724, in Königsberg, Prussia. His ancestors were originally Scotch; and although he was but the son of a saddler, he received a good education. His parents were Pietists; and, as one might consequently suppose, he was brought up under strongly religious influences. Kant's mother was a woman known for her modesty, uprightness, and piety, and he inherited those qualities from her.

He was, therefore, also deliberate and serious-minded. His daily life was so well regulated that he was said to be more punctual than a clock. He taught mathematics, physics, geography, logic, ethics, and metaphysics at the university in Königsberg, holding his position to an old age.

His masterpiece, the *Critique of Pure Reason*, was published in 1781. Once published, it thrilled the philosophical world of the day, and many scholars came to pay homage to him. His entire life was spent within the boundaries of his native city. He never married, and actually lived the life of a hermit. Although delicate in health, he observed a moderation that helped him to reach the age of eighty. He died in 1804.

Kant engaged in writing until his last years, and it is a marvel that his brain was active for so long. When he died, his body appeared to be all dried up—a mere mass of skin and bone.

Although his works are innumerable, besides the *Critique of Pure Reason*, we may mention here his *Critique of Practical Reason* (1788), and the *Critique of Judgment* (1790). Kant rejected dogmatism and skepticism, and sought truth by the critical method. He held that the content of experience comes from sense perception, but that its form is given *a priori*, and comes from the activity of the mind itself.

He was a model for scholars, and in his character and activity there was nothing to be criticized. Modern philosophy, initiated by Descartes, culminated in Kant.

Further Reading. The articles about Kant in the *Stanford Encyclopedia of Philosophy* (plato.stanford.edu) and the *Internet Encyclopedia of Philosophy* (iep.utm.edu) do no good work in relativizing the picture of the rigid "clockwork Kant" that we encountered above, but they are otherwise helpful. The book *Kant: A Biography* by Manfred KUEHN (orig. Germ., Cambridge UP, 2011), which, with its 576 pages, can also serve as an easy to follow introduction to Kant's thinking, portrays a man who was, during most of his life, a highly sociable and elegant gentleman who valued friendship, and whose esprit as a conservationist was appreciated everywhere in Königsberg's high society. When intending to learn about Kantian philosophy, it is advisable to first consider whether one is interested in theoretical problems or ethics. In case of the former, the book by Jay F. ROSENBERG, *Accessing Kant: A Relaxed Introduction to the Critique of Pure Reason* (Oxford UP, 2005), might be a good way to start. Taking up the challenge to read the *Critique of Pure Reason* oneself, it is recommended that, after reading the introductions (1st ed. 1871, 2nd ed. 1787), one continues with the "Transcendental Doctrine of Method," which is the last part of the book. The reader may then reflect again whether he really wants to delve into the complexities of Kant's epistemology, or prefers to proceed with his practical philosophy. In the latter case, the *Groundwork of the Metaphysics of Morals* (1785) is the text to begin with. Parallelly, one may consult the book by Jennifer K. ULEMAN, *An Introduction to Kant's Moral Philosophy* (Cambridge UP, 2010). Due to the difficulty of Kant's philosophical writings, it is not recommendable to work with older translations, even if they are accessible online. The new standard English edition of Kant's writings is the *Cambridge Edition of the Works of Immanuel Kant*, edited by Paul GUYER and Allen W. WOOD (Cambridge UP, 1992 ongoing).

2. The Six Wise Men of the East

Name	Inscription	Reading	Meaning
Shōtoku Taishi	聖徳太子	*Shōtoku Taishi*	Prince of Holy Virtue
Sugawara no Michizane	菅公	*Kan-kō*	Official Sedge
Zhuāngzǐ	莊子	*Zhuāngzǐ*	Solemn Master
Zhū Xī	朱熹	*Zhū Xī*	Cinnabar Light
Nāgārjuna	龍樹大士	*Ryūju-daiji*	Great Master Serpent Tree
Kapila	迦毘羅仙	*Kapira-sen*	Hermit Kapila

Shotoku Taishi

Prince Shōtoku, the first son of the Emperor Employing Clarity (Yōmei), was born in the year 572 CE. His genius became apparent at an early age. In his childhood he showed great interest in books, especially in those on Buddhism. Prince Shōtoku and the chancellor Soga Umako were, in fact, the first faithful followers of Buddhism in Japan. At that time, Mononobe no Moriya, a rival of the Soga clan, desired to drive Buddhism from Japan. He waged war on Soga, but he was defeated and met with death. Buddhism flourished after that, and grew to such an extent that forty-six temples were erected and more than one thousand three hundred and eighty priests were ordained. All of this took place in one generation.

聖徳
用明
蘇我馬子
物部守屋

Prince Shōtoku was fond of cultivating the friendship of naturalized foreigners and known scholars. He eagerly absorbed aspects of their different civilizations, and open-mindedly studied their world-views, thereby gaining a basis for his political insight. Thus, when Empress Promoting Antiquity (Suiko) ascended the throne as successor to Emperor Employing Clarity, she named Prince Shōtoku as regent and consigned the entire administration to his care. He was then able to display the holy sublimity of his character. In foreign affairs, he displayed national power; in domestic matters, he broke the power of the clans. Meanwhile, he perfected his principles of the holiness of the Imperial Household and the centralization of the Empire.

推古

冠位十二階

十七條憲法

As Prince Regent he established Twelve Court Ranks as well as the so-called Seventeen Article Constitution, the directives of which are here briefly listed:

1. To establish harmony 和.
2. To hold in reverence the Buddha, the Dharma, and the Sangha (i.e., the Three Jewels).
3. To strictly observe the Imperial Order.
4. For all officials to make propriety 禮 their daily standard.
5. Through discretion and contentment, to judge all struggles with fairness of mind.
6. To repulse evil and promote the good 懲惡勸善.
7. As each one has his own duty to perform, for each office there is the right person.
8. For each official to attend his offices early and withdraw therefrom late.
9. Sincerity being the ethical foundation, for each to strive to be sincere 信.
10. To refrain from anger at the errors of others.
11. To distinguish between merit and fault, and to distribute reward and punishment fairly.
12. For the governor not to unduly tax the farmer.
13. For an official to know and pursue his own function.
14. For officials not to envy one another.

15. For public 公 interests to come first, private 私 second.
16. To levy the subjects as best fits the seasons.
17. To shun dogmatic action, and to widely discuss 論 important issues.

As can be seen, the seventeen articles comprise precious maxims. Also extant to this day are Prince Shōtoku's *Commentaries of the Three Sūtras* which are the *Lotus Sūtra* (Jp. *Hokke-kyō*), the *Queen Śrīmālā Sūtra* (Jp. *Shōma-gyō*), and the *Vimalakīrti Sūtra* (Jp. *Yuima-gyō*).

三經義流
法華經
勝鬘經
維摩經

When the Prince fell ill, an Imperial messenger came to ask what his last will might be. He expressed his wish that Buddhism may flourish, that temples be built and maintained, and that the Imperial dynasty be protected and revered in eternity. He died at the age of forty-nine, in the year 621, at the Grosbeak Palace (*Ikaruga-no-miya*) in the Nara Capital. He was buried in the Long Scarp Mound (*Shinaga-no-misasagi*), and everyone lamented his death as if it were that of a parent—it is said that the sobs of the people were heard everywhere. He is known by many names (Prince Umayado, Toyotomimi, and Kamitsumiya), but he was commonly known as Shōtoku Taishi, i.e., Prince Shōtoku. Shōtoku means "holy and benevolent," which corresponds to his real character.

斑鳩宮
磯長陵
厩戸　豊聡耳
上宮
聖徳太子

Further Reading. There is a concise but informative article—including a bibliography—about the (in all aspects) historically contested figure of Shōtoku Taishi in the *Encyclopedia of Buddhism* (ed. R. E. Buswell, Macmillan, 2003). A translation of the Seventeen Article Constitution, together with related source materials, can be found in the "Prince Shōtoku and his Constitution" chapter in the first volume of the *Sources of Japanese Tradition* (ed. W. T. de Bary et al., 2nd. ed., Columbia UP,

2002). The monograph by Michael Como, *Shōtoku: Ethnicity, Ritual, and Violence in the Japanese Buddhist Tradition* (Oxford UP, 2006), rather than hypothesizing about Prince Shōtoku's historical authenticity, focuses instead on the emergence of the legend and cult of this Japanese cultural hero.

Sugawara no Michizane

道眞　是善
菅原

Michizane, the third son of Chancellor Koreyoshi of the Sedgeland (Sugawara) clan, was born in 845 CE. From infancy he surpassed all others. His learning progressed with the years, and he received the degree of Doctor of Literature, the highest honor in learning at that time. He was also rapidly promoted in his government positions, until he finally became Minister to the Emperor and occupied the right seat, with Tokihira of the Wisteriafield (Fujiwara) clan occupying the left. Michizane's fame spread far and wide, and he grew to be the Emperor's favorite. Slandered by Tokihira, his rival, in the end he was exiled from the capital to the Great Headquarters (Dazaifu) on Full Domain (Kyūshū) island. He died there in 903 CE, at the age of fifty-eight.

藤原時平

太宰府
九州

Michizane was fond of the apricot blossom. When going into exile, he wrote a poem to this flower that became popular. Translated, it goes as follows:

東風吹かば匂いおこせよ梅の花主無しとて春を忘るな

When the East wind blows,
O Apricot Blossom, forget not the Spring tide;
But send me thy perfume,
Tho' thy master be gone.

Upon his removal to the Great Headquarters, he closed the gate to his residence and never set foot outside of it as long as he lived. He overrode his mental torture with his literary efforts, among which we have the following well-known lines, as they are freely rendered here:

去年今夜待清涼 *'Til a year this night since,*
I attended the Emperor's ceremony at Purity Palace.

秋思詩篇獨斷腸 *At thought of these verses on Autumn meditation,*
My quivering heart into torture is plunged.

恩賜御衣今在此 *The court garb, a gift from my noble Emperor,*
My prize of that night, lies before me.

捧持毎日拜餘香 *Bowing over this Imperial dress,*
I sense the fragrance of his kindly spirit.

Sugawara no Michizane excelled in the art of poetry; his poems are still extant. With other scholars, he collected the fifty volumes of the *Chronicle of Three Regencies*. And at the behest of an Imperial Order, he classified the old history of Japan, compiling two hundred volumes called, *Compiled National History*.

三代實録

類聚國史

He took faith in Buddhism and, upon hearing the divine teachings of the *Lotus Sūtra*, he believed that faith is in itself Buddhahood and that the common people are themselves Buddha. He said: "In Buddha there is no coming and going, no before and no after. If sincerity exists, how is it that Buddha is not found in all homes? There is only one soul; Dharma alone exists."[38] He clothed the same underlying religious feeling, with its ethical significance, in Shintoist thought as follows:[39]

法華經

38 I was unable to verify the authenticity of this quotation added by Genichi.

39 Translated by Nitobe Inazō [Nitobé Inazo] 新渡戸稲造, in his book *The*

心だに誠の道にかなひなば祈らず とても神や守らん	*The god blesseth* *Not him who prayeth* *But him whose heart strayeth* *Not from the way of truthfulness*

He supported the one-source doctrine of loyalty and piety. He contended that "the teachings of the Emperor and of the father should be one. At the gate of filial devotion there is also loyalty to the Emperor. There is no difference in the path of the true subject and of the son."[40] Although he was born of a family of Confucian scholars, he himself recognized the beauty of the national spirit. In one of his writings on this subject we find the following lines:[41]

凡神國一世無窮玄妙者不可敢而窺知雖學漢土三代周孔之聖經革命之國風深可加思慮也	The infinity and sublimity of the sacred land is shrouded in a veil of mystery. Although we study the divine Chinese books of the Three Dynasties [Xià 夏, Shāng 商, and Zhōu 周 recorded by Prince] Zhōu and Confucius, the revolutionary background of the Chinese people must be carefully weighed.
凡國學所要雖欲論涉古今究天人其自非和魏漢才不能闞其閫奥矣	The goal of Japanese learning is the study of heaven and mankind from ancient time to modern; but we cannot attain this goal without Japanese Soul and Chinese talents.

Japanese Nation: Its Land, Its People, and Its Life (New York: G. P. Putnam's Sons, 1912), p. 133. The Japanese word *makoto* has been substituted with "truthfulness."

40 I was unable to verify the authenticity of this quotation added by Genichi.

41 『菅家遺誡』[Bequeathed instructions by the Suga clan]. Ascribed to Sugawara no Michizane, but likely to be apocryphal.

These wise sayings fully illustrate his superior insight, and also exemplify, as does Shōtoku Taishi, the attitude of a wise Japanese statesman in introducing foreign civilization. Michizane's knowledge and virtues are held in high esteem. After his death, shrines to his memory as the God of Learning and Calligraphy were erected all over Japan. Aided by the superstitious belief in his vengeance, and by sympathy for the unjust fate that befell him in spite of his loyalty, the scholar's spirit is also worshiped under the name Deity of Heaven's Full [Wrath]. 天満天神

Further Reading. Western research on Sugawara no Michizane was conducted by Robert Borgen. His article giving basic biographical information appears in the *Kodansha Encyclopedia of Japan* (1983–1986). In the *Cambridge History of Japanese Literature* (ed. H. Shirane et al., 2016), he introduces Sugawara's significance as poet and literati. Last but not least there is his monograph, *Sugawara no Michizane and the Early Heian Court* (Hawaii UP, 1994)—the standard work on this historical figure.

Zhuangzi

Zhuāngzǐ, born at Méng in the third or the fourth century of the Common Era, was a contemporary of Mencius. His works are mostly allegorical, and his ideas, based on those of Lǎozǐ, were opposed to the doctrine of Confucius. King Dignity (Ch. Wēi) of the Chǔ State, hearing favorable reports of Zhuāngzǐ's sagacity, sent messengers to him to welcome him to the Chǔ State and to offer him

莊子　蒙

老子

威　楚

the post of Prime Minister. At this, Zhuāngzǐ smiled and said to the messengers:

> You offer me great wealth and a proud position indeed; but have you never seen a sacrificial ox?— When after being fattened up for several years, it is decked with embroidered trappings and led to the altar, would it not willingly then change places with some uncared-for pigling? … Begone! Defile me not! I would rather disport myself to my own enjoyment in the mire than be slave to the ruler of a State. I will never take office. Thus I shall remain free to follow my own inclinations.[42]

With such words, he declined the offer; and at no time did he serve in any government capacity—all of which shows that his goal was high. His works are numerous:[43]

"Transcendental Bliss"「逍遙遊」
"The Identity of Contraries"「齊物論」
"Nourishment of the Soul"「養生主」
"Man among Men"「人間世」
"The Evidence of Virtue Complete"「德充符」
"The Great Supreme"「大宗師」
"How to Govern"「應帝王」

Exquisitely beautiful, and profound in nature, his literary style could well be called transcendent. However deep the learning of Lǎozǐ may have been, it could not have been disseminated without Zhuāngzǐ. His readers have always admired his fine and enchanting literary style, but not the mysticism of his principles. The reason for this is that

42 Translation taken from *Chuang Tzŭ: Mystic, Moralist, and Social Reformer,* trans. by Herbert A. Giles (London: Bernhard Quaritch, 1889), pp. vi–vii.

43 Genichi here gives the titles of the seven so-called "inner chapters" 內篇 of the book which is traditionally attributed to Zhuāngzǐ. He cites again the translation by Giles (see note 42) which is not recommended anymore.

they gauge his essays from the standpoint of Confucianism. If seen from a metaphysical viewpoint, the profundity of his thought is even superior to his literary style. His doctrines stressed the power of silence and quietism, complete detachment, solitude, inaction, life and death blended into one, as well as the unification of right and wrong: "thus shall we glimpse the depths of mysticism in the universe and gaze upon the light of the Absolute."[44] Thus are we left to judge the greatness of Zhuāngzǐ, the individual who expounded such principles.

Further Reading. The *Stanford Encyclopedia of Philosophy* (plato.stanford.edu) has an excellent, albeit very technical article on the book *Zhuāngzǐ*. The article in the *Internet Encyclopedia of Philosophy* (iep.utm.edu) is limited to the classic's seven so-called "inner chapters," as are many of its translations. Rather than through introductions, it is recommended to approach this text—which is among the most celebrated literary and philosophical products of the Chinese tradition—by reading it oneself. The classical translation by James Legge, published 1891 in volumes 39 and 40 of the *Sacred Books of the East* (ed. M. Müller, Clarendon Press), can be found as digital text included in the Chinese Text Project (ctext.org), and as scan in the Internet Archive (archive.org). The other complete translation that can be recommended is *The Complete Works of Chuang Tzu* (Columbia UP, 1968), by Burton Watson.

44 I was unable to verify the authenticity of this quotation added by Genichi.

Zhu Xi

朱熹　宋
尤溪
福建

孝經

八卦

劉勉之

高宗

寧宗

Zhū Xī of the Sòng dynasty, known as Master Zhū, was born around 1130 CE, in Superb Valley (Yóuxī), in today's Fortune Building (Fújiàn) Province. At the age of five, while in elementary school, he mastered and recited the *Classic of Filial Piety*, which deals with filial duties. The genius in him inspired him to write these words on the cover of the book: "If I cannot conform to these lessons, I shall never be a man." When at play, he would form the "eight trigrams" of human fate with grains of sand; and he would amuse himself by gazing upon this work. He was mentored by Liú Miǎnzhī. Recognizing his extraordinary talents, Liú Miǎnzhī desired him as a son-in-law.

During the reign of Emperor Eminent Founder (Gāozōng), Zhū Xī passed the difficult examination required of government officials and served with the local administration. Gradually, his fame spread. His persevering industry and the increase of his learning added greatly to his renown, which finally shone forth like a guiding star for the entire world to follow. The court instructor advised the Emperor that if one sought to acquire the principles of good conduct and cultured learning, it would be well to employ the first among men. By "first among men," he meant Zhū Xī.

Some time later, during the reign of the Emperor Calm Founder (Nìngzōng), he was invited to the court at the request of the Emperor; but there he was accused of sophistry by the opposition parties. He was dismissed after forty-six days of service at court. He withdrew from court life and spent his time giving lectures to his pupils.

In the year 1201 CE, he fell ill. At the age of seventy-one, on the day of his death, he sat erect and adjusted his head-gear and dress. Even in his last moments, leaning against the pillows, he indicated the desire for paper and a pen-brush to his attendants. But, too weak to move his hand, he then died.

His funeral was attended by thousands of mourners, in spite of the influence not to do so exerted by his opponents. This shows how extensively his merits influenced the minds of the people. His glory later became so great that he was enshrined at the side of Confucius in the Confucian Temple.

Without becoming dogmatic, Zhū Xī based his philosophical doctrine on the old Chinese dualistic cosmogony. Before determining moral law, he extensively researched the laws of the world as put forward by preceding philosophers. He systematized their teachings, and from them created a fine ethical standard. His doctrines promoted self-cultivation and practical social good in China, Korea, and Japan.

FURTHER READING. Both the *Internet Encyclopedia of Philosophy* (iep.utm.edu) and the *Stanford Encyclopedia of Philosophy* (plato.stanford.edu) have an article about the foundational thinker of Neo-Confucianism. While the article in the Stanford Encyclopedia, including its bibliography, is the more comprehensive, the Internet Encyclopedia's article is more readable for the non-expert, and has a selected bibliography that is helpfully commented. If one is not particularly interested in Zhū Xī's metaphysics, the most proficient way to approach this thinker is to read the four ancient books—*Confucian Analects*, *Mencius*, *Great Learning*, and *Doctrine of the Mean*—which Zhū Xī commented on and established as the scholarly paradigm that swayed East Asian secular education until the modern era. The classical translations by James LEGGE from 1861 largely follow Zhū Xī's commentary. They can be found as digital text included in the Chinese Text Project (ctext.org), and as scan in the Internet Archive (archive.org).[45] Zhū Xī's prefaces to the Great Learning and the Doctrine of the Mean are among the most influential of his programmatic writings. Translations of the prefaces, together with excerpts from the respective books and Zhū Xī's commentaries, are compiled in volume one (pp. 720–37) of *Sources of Chinese Tradition* (ed. W. T. de BARY et al., 2nd ed., Columbia UP, 1999).

Nagarjuna

After the death of Śākyamuni Buddha, Hīnayāna Buddhism alone prevailed and, according to various chronicles, split into twenty to five hundred sects whose principles differed only by degrees. This division into many sects, a deviation from Buddha's original ideas, resulted in the decline of Buddhism around the beginning of the Common Era. At the end of the second century, Aśvaghoṣa, and later Nāgārjuna, reanimated Buddhism. Aśvaghoṣa's efforts, being in the transitional period between Hīnayāna and Mahāyāna, shows Hīnayāna as well as Mahāyāna tendencies, but Nāgārjuna's work represents pure Mahāyāna.[46]

45 The translations from 1861, published as volumes one and two of James Legge's *Chinese Classics* series (London: Trubner), were reprinted "with few alterations" (Preface, 1893) in the revised editions of 1893 and 1895 (Oxford: Clarendon Press).

46 Since Sanskrit *hīna-yāna* (lesser vehicle) has a pejorative meaning, modern scholars use the term Theravāda Buddhism.

Nāgārjuna was born of the Brahmin caste in South India, around the end of the second or the beginning of the third century. Intelligent by nature, even in his childhood he composed forty thousand poems while hearing others recite the four Vedas. In his youth he mastered every science of the times, including astronomy, geography, medicine, and mathematics. His fame spread far and wide. In his arrogance he thought that he could gratify all of his desires, and, losing his way, gave himself up to lustful pleasures along with his friends. Afterward repentant, he joined the Buddhist priesthood and studied all the Hīnayāna Sūtras. The tenets of these teachings giving him no satisfaction, he sought to find a new religion. Legend has it that he found the Mahāyāna Sūtras in a dragon-castle, and that he mastered all of them. Scholars assume that place to have been located in a northern district in one of the mountain ranges running from the Pamir Plateau. Returning to South India, Nāgārjuna died around the end of the third century. Āryadeva was his great disciple. Nāgārjuna is said to have written the following works:

"Five Thousand Verses on the Treatise about Compassionate Means"『大悲方便論五千偈』
"Five Thousand Verses on the Great Adornment Treatise"『大莊嚴論五千偈』
"One Hundred Thousand Verses on the Treatise on Great Fearlessness"『大無畏論十萬偈』
"One Hundred Thousand Verses on Instruction"『優波提舍論十萬偈』[47]

47 Enryō may have taken this list from『佛祖統紀』[Comprehensive chronicle of the Buddha and patriarchs] (T 2035, 49: 174). I am not sure, however, whether these texts even exist.

Extant works attributed to Nāgārjuna in the Chinese canon are:

"Treatise on Great Transcending Wisdom"『大智度論』(Skt. *Mahāprajñāpāramitā-śāstra*)
"Treatise on the Middle Way"『中論』(Skt. *Madhyamaka-kārikā*)
"Treatise of the Twelve Aspects"『十二門論』(Skt. *Dvādaśanikāya-śāstra*)
"Explanatory Treatise on the Twelve Stages"『十住毘婆沙論』(Skt. *Daśabhūmika-vibhāṣā-śāstra*).

From Nāgārjuna's writings one may learn the principles of Mahāyāna Buddhism. The essence of his teaching is the revelation of the Absolute through the negation of all relative conceptions. Hīnayāna, in contrast, although negating phenomena, maintains the relative concept of universal being. Furthermore, as the natural outcome of his idea of the Absolute, Nāgārjuna conceived of an all-saving Buddha, which contrasts with the Hīnayāna goal of self-contentment. Mahāyāna Buddhism was introduced in Japan through China, and developed its religious aspect here.

Nāgārjuna's principles are little known among western peoples, as most of his teachings are accessible only through Chinese translations. Nāgārjuna well deserves his epithets: the Ancestor of the Eight Sects, the Reviver of Buddhism, and the Second Buddha.

Further Reading. The text above is correct in its emphasis of the importance of this Buddhist philosopher, but it is highly misleading in terms of the current state of research. Among the works mentioned, only the authorship of the *Treatise on the Middle Way* (*Madhyamaka-kārikā*), is uncontested. Nāgārjuna's key doctrinal term, emptiness

(Skt. *śūnyatā*), is not even mentioned. And it is doubtful whether the historical person Nāgārjuna had any interest in the swelling Mahāyāna movement of his time. Both the *Internet Encyclopedia of Philosophy* (iep.utm.edu) and the *Stanford Encyclopedia of Philosophy* (plato.stanford.edu) have an article on Nāgārjuna. While the former is more readable for the non-expert, the latter includes a good bibliography which lists translations "that are particularly accessible to philosophers without specialized training in Indology." Three translations of the *Madhyamaka-kārikā*, the most important of Nāgārjuna's philosophical works, are also among the translations listed. In the Thesaurus Literaturae Buddhicae, which is part of the digital Bibliotheca Polyglotta (www2.hf.uio.no/polyglotta), the text can be read in English translation while comparing the Sanskrit, Tibetan, and Chinese versions.

Kapila

In India, the philosophies following the Brahmin religion were divided into six large schools, among which the Sāṃkhya school was philosophically foremost.[48] Kapila means "yellow-red." Maybe Kapila was thus named because his hair or complexion was of this color. His dates are unknown; however, it is certain that he lived before Śākyamuni Buddha.

According to legends from Chinese sources, Kapila appeared either at the chaotic beginning of the world, or was born from *śūnya* (emptiness or void). The sources

48 The other five are Yoga, Pūrva-Mīmāṃsā (focused on the earlier Vedic texts), Vedānta (or Uttara-Mīmāṃsā, focused on the later Vedic texts, i.e., the Upaniṣad), as well as the Vaiśeṣika, which is closely associated with the logical Nyāya. About Nyāya, *see below* under Akṣapāda.

also report that the hermit Kapila was naturally endowed with four virtues: justice, wisdom, contentment, and freedom. Out of compassion for the world, he taught the "twenty-five elements" to Āsuri, who transmitted the teaching to Pañcaśikha. Kapila's teachings eventually came to be known by Īśvarakṛṣṇa, who compiled them as the *Sāṃkhya Treatise* (Skt. *Sāṃkhya-kārikā*), which is the earliest and most important textbook of the school.

The twenty-five elements as taught in the Sāṃkhya system are:

1.	Matter (Skt. *prakṛti*)
2.	Perception (Skt. *manas*)
3.	Ego (Skt. *ahaṃkāra*)
4 to 8.	Five Qualities: Color, Sound, Smell, Taste, and Touch.
9 to 13.	Five Senses: Visual, Auditory, Olfactory, Gustatory, and Tactile.
14 to 18.	Five Actions: Actions of Tongue, Hands, Feet, Sex, and Body in general.
19 to 23.	Five Elements: Earth, Water, Fire, Wind, and Ether.
24.	Intellect (Skt. *buddhi*)
25.	Soul (Skt. *puruṣa*)

This is the ontology of the Sāṃkhya system. Of these elements, the first and the last, Matter and Soul, exist inherently. The development of the other twenty-three elements is dependent upon these two. Matter has movement, but Soul does not. Matter is ignorance, but Soul is knowledge. The former is thus active and unknowing, while the latter is passive and immobile. So the union of Matter and Soul is a union of the unknowing and the immobile. Sāṃkhya thusly explains the cause of darkness and suffering. Salvation is attained by knowledge of the original distinctiveness of Matter and Soul. The Soul becomes steady and free through awareness of its original independence.

Thus, we learn of the greatness of mind and character of the philosopher Kapila from the philosophy that his principles brought about rather than from facts concerning his life.

FURTHER READING. As in the case of Akṣapāda (see below), the name Kapila stands more for a school of Indian philosophy than for an historical person, as nothing can be known with certainty about the legendary founder of the Sāṃkhya system. An article in the *Internet Encyclopedia of Philosophy* (iep.utm.edu) gives a good summary of Sāṃkhya thought. A complete translation of the *Sāṃkhya-kārikā*, the foundational text of the Sāṃkhya school, can be found in the Appendix of the study by Gerald J. LARSON, *Classical Sāṃkhya: An Interpretation of its History and Meaning* (2nd. rev. ed., Motilal Banarsidass, 1979). Larson's translation is also the basis for the summary in volume four of the *Encyclopedia of Indian Philosophies* (ed. G. J. LARSON et al., Princeton UP, 1987). Both works are accessible online in the Internet Archive (archive.org).

3. The Three Founders of Philosophy

Name	Inscription	Reading	Meaning
Yellow Emperor	黄帝	*Huángdì*	Yellow Emperor
Akṣapāda	足目	*Sokumoku*	Foot Eyed One
Thales	多禮	*Tarei[su]*	Manifold Reverent One

The Yellow Emperor

志那黄帝	Yellow Emperor of China
黄帝小傳 傳曰黄帝有熊氏名軒轅生而神靈長而聰明察五氣立五運順天地之紀定幽明之占	Abridged Legend of the Yellow Emperor Tradition speaks thus of the Yellow Emperor: His family name was Bernard (Yǒuxióng). His personal name Charioteer (Xuānyuán). He was born with a Divine Spirit. He was bred in wisdom. He perceived the Five Elements. He established the Five Rounds of Evolution. He followed the order of Heaven and Earth. He guided the destinies of this life and that of the next.
叉曰帝與歧伯上窮天紀下極地理遠取諸物近取諸身更相問難而作內經	Tradition also says: The Emperor, with court physician Qí, investigated the order of Heaven, expounded the theory of the Earth, culled knowledge from out of matter, culled knowledge from the Self. Thus they reasoned together and created the philosophical cabala.

蓋支那哲學發源於此其後歷千有餘年百家競起一盛二衰以至今日黄帝實爲其肇祖焉	Chinese philosophy started out from there. In the course of the thousand and more years since then, hundreds of philosophers have arisen and contended with each other. Of their teachings some flourished, some decayed. And thus it continues to this day. The Yellow Emperor is indeed the founding father of Chinese philosophy.
右黄帝小傳 井上圓了識	This is the abridged legend of the Yellow Emperor. Recorded by Inoue Enryō
田中良雄鐫	Carved by Tanaka Yoshio

Further Reading. An article in the *Encyclopedia of Taoism* (ed. F. Pregadio, Routledge, 2008) tells of the philological sources of the myth of the Yellow Emperor, and points to further research. The article immediately following the entry on the Yellow Emperor is about the text which Genichi rendered as the "philosophical cabala" and in Chinese is called *Inner Guideline of the Yellow Emperor*. This work, mythologically attributed to the Yellow Emperor, is the classic of Chinese medical theory. Recent research on the myth of the Yellow Emperor, whose significance goes far beyond that of being a Daoist deity, can be found in volume three of the *Journal of Chinese Humanities* (1st issue, 2017). The issue contains two articles by Chinese philologists about the emergence and development of the Yellow Emperor narrative.

黄帝內經

Aksapada

印度足目	Akṣapāda of India
足目小傳 足目者印度古仙也不詳其年代或云劫初大梵天王化作此仙或云其人既帝天也兩說荒唐不可信據然此仙遠在迦以前始說因明法	Abridged Legend of Akṣapāda Akṣapāda was an old Indian hermit; there seems to be no chronological data available concerning him. It is said that, when the cosmos was still in a nebulous state, the King of the Brahman Heaven was reincarnated in the shape of Akṣapāda. Other sources maintain that this philosopher is the supreme Deity Brahman, Himself. One can give little credit to these vague and groundless legends. Still it is true that Akṣapāda lived years before the Buddha. He was the first Indian scholar to teach logic and epistemology.
立九句因及十四過類是爲論理之規短爾來諸學派皆由此以判是非辨邪那正故今推足目爲印度哲學鼻祖也	He expounded the Nine Examples and also the Fourteen Fallacies, which formed the basis of his logic. Since his time, every school of Indian philosophy has followed his logic, which judges true and false and distinguishes between right and wrong. For this reason, I take Akṣapāda as the founder of Indian philosophy.
右足目小傳 井上圓了識	This is the abridged legend of Akṣapāda. Recorded by Inoue Enryō
田中良雄鐫	Carved by Tanaka Yoshio

FURTHER READING. As the inscription on the Three Founders Monument suggests, Akṣapāda is a legendary figure about which nothing is known with certainty. He is taken to be the author of the *Nyāya-sūtra*, which is the basic text of the Nyāya school—the logical school among the six orthodox Hindu philosophies.[49] Volume

49 The others are Sāṃkhya, Yoga, Pūrva-Mīmāṃsā (focused on the earlier Vedic texts), Vedānta (focused on the later Vedic texts, i.e., the Upaniṣad), and Vaiśeṣika, which is closely associated with Nyāya.

two of the *Encyclopedia of Indian Philosophies* (ed. K. H. Potter, Princeton UP, 1977) provides a summary of the *sūtra*, which took its final form during the first two or three centuries of the Common Era. Bibliographical information and a general introduction to Indian logic are given in the article on Nyāya in the *Internet Encyclopedia of Philosophy* (iep.utm.edu).

Thales

西洋多禮	Thales of the West
多禮須小傳 往古希臘有七賢 人多體須居其首 位西曆紀元前七 世紀之人夙究數 學兼修星學進破 當時神話依物理 原則溯天地太初 竟以水爲世界眞 元森羅萬象管生 於水云	Abridged Legend of Thales In ancient times in Greece, there were Seven Sages. Thales was the first among them all. He lived in the seventh century before Christ. During his early period, he meditated upon mathematics as well as astronomy. He strove to destroy belief in mythology. Based on physical laws, he traced the origin of Heaven and Earth. Considering water the origin of the world, he held that all phenomena are born out of water.
自是而後諸家輩 出甲論乙駁遂成 西洋哲學大觀矣 然始開其端者即 多體須其人也	Since then many thinkers have appeared, argued with each other, and reasoned about this. Out of these discussions, the great vista of Occidental philosophy arose. And it was none other than Thales who initiated this development.
右多禮須小傳 井上圓了識	This is the abridged legend of Thales. Recorded by Inoue Enryō
田中良雄鐫	Carved by Tanaka Yoshio

Further Reading. After Thales von Milet, the others of the Seven Sages mentioned in the text are commonly listed as Cleobulus of Lindos, Solon of Athens, Chilon of Sparta, Pittacus of Mytilene, and Bias of Priene (all around 600 BCE). The article about Thales in the *Internet Encyclopedia of Philosophy* (iep.utm.edu) is optimistic in terms of historicity, but is to the same degree also informative. The extant testimonies about Thales can be found in volume one of *The Texts of Early Greek Philosophy: The Complete Fragments and Selected Testimonies of the Major Presocratics*, edited and translated by Daniel W. Graham (Cambridge UP, 2010).

4. The Three Japanese Erudites

Name	Inscription	Reading	Meaning
Hirata Atsutane	平田篤胤大人	*Hirata Atsutane Ushi*	Great Sincere Seed of Evenfield
Hayashi Razan	林羅山先生	*Hayashi Razan Sensei*	Master Grove of Silk Mountain
Gyōnen	釋凝然大徳	*Shaku Gyōnen Daitoku*	Abiding One of Great Virtue of the Śākya [Clan]

Hirata Atsutane

The Great (*ushi*) Hirata Atsutane (1776–1843), is a giant among the scholars of Japan. His childhood name was Right Fortune, his common name Wide Angle. He was born in 1776, in the castle town Autumn Field (Akita), in Spreading Wings (Dewa) province. His father was a domain samurai of the Supporting Bambus (Satake) clan. At the age of eight, Hirata began with Chinese studies, and after that he was trained in medicine. By the age of eleven, he made up his mind and decided to give up his studies and leave his home province. With the small sum of money of only one tael (Jp. *ryō*), he went on a journey, overcame all hardship, and finally arrived in River Hamlet (i.e., Edo, today's Tokyo). Independent and sovereign, without support from his domain, and having no friends, all he wanted was to find a good teacher to follow. Floating around for four or five years, he did not care about his misery or even about the hardship of sustaining himself.

大人　平田篤胤
正吉　大角
秋田
出羽
佐竹
兩
江戸

平田
備中
本居宣長
眞菅乃屋
氣吹乃屋
石

Fortunately, in 1800, he was adopted as heir by the Evenfield (Hirata) clan of Bicchū province, and so he had a place to live in River Hamlet.

In 1801, he read a book by Motoori Norinaga for the first time, and he had a great awakening. From that time, he put all of his efforts into the promotion of the old ways. In 1804, he changed his home to Real Sedge Dwelling (*Masuge-no-ya*), and opened his doors for students in order to teach them. Thereafter, he wrote books every year for the restoration of old ways. He changed his school again, to Odem Hut (*Ibuki-no-ya*), and word of his fame became heard near and far. He was allowed to present his works to the court in Kyoto, and upon doing so received an income of one hundred *koku* of rice (ca. 180 liters) from the Autumn Field domain. Hirata returned to Autumn Field in 1843, and fell sick soon after. At day eleven of the ninth month of the same year, he became guest to the world of the dead. He was 68 years old.

神靈能眞柱大人

The achievement of his lifetime was to invigorate old learning. He bequeathed more than one hundred writings, and the number of his students reached more than one thousand. It was through him that Shinto had a great ascension. Therefore, he must be seen as an exceptionally great man. In 1845, he was bestowed the posthumous title Great August Pillar of the Spirits (*Kamutama-no-mihashira-no-ushi*).

Further Reading. The online *Encyclopedia of Shinto* (eos.kokugakuin.ac.jp) provides basic and reliable information about Hirata Atsutane, but does not lead the Western reader to further literature. The only in-depth study in English about Hirata's life and the development of his school is the monograph by Mark McNally, titled,

Proving the Way: Conflict and Practice in the History of Japanese Nativism (Harvard UP, 2005). The *Sources of Japanese Tradition* (ed. W. T. de BARY et al., 2nd. ed., Columbia UP, 2002) contains several short excerpts from Hirata's works in English. The sourcebook, *Japanese Philosophy* (ed. J. W. HEISIG et al., Hawaii UP, 2011), has a twelve-page extract from Hirata's important work, *The True Pillar of the Soul.* 靈能眞柱

Hayashi Razan

Hayashi Nobukatsu, or HAYASHI Razan (1583–1657), was born in 1583. He was a Confucian official of the Tokugawa regime. His ancestors were from Blessington (Kaga), and later moved to Long Region (Kishū). His father came to live in Kyoto. Master Razan was born an exceptional talent. He had heard someone reading the *Chronicle of Great Peace* when he was eight years old, and had immediately memorized it. After this incident, everyone called him a wonder child. At the age of fourteen, he entered the Temple of Building Kindness (Kennin-ji) in order to study. However, it was a time of military turmoil, and therefore difficult to acquire books. He looked for books in all directions; when he got his hands on one every once in a while, he would read it in one night.

林信勝　羅山
加賀
紀州
太平記
建仁寺

Growing up in this manner, he inquired ever more widely into the teachings of all schools. It was said that there was almost nothing composed of letters that he had not read. What he came to revere the most were the Six Classics and—in order to grasp their gist—the works of the Chéng brothers and Zhū Xī. Eventually, he opened a school and taught the theories of Sòng-Confucianism.

六經
程　朱熹

藤原惺窩

徳川家康

將軍

剃髪　道春

民部卿法印

Around this time, he revered and became the student of Fujiwara Seika, who lived—withdrawn—in the north of the capital. As he plumbed the meaning of the classics even further, Tokugawa Ieyasu heard of his reputation and sent for him. In 1606, he was given a doctorate and put in the position of an adviser to the General (*shōgun*). Thereafter, he called himself Boldhead, or Spring of the Path, and was appointed the rank of Seal of Law of the People's Ministry. He enjoyed great confidence, and he even drafted a law for the court council. He died in 1657, on day 23 of the first month, during the fourth generation of Tokugawa rule. He lived for 75 years (according to pre-modern Japanese age counting).

信勝

羅山

文敏

His given name was Eloquence (Nobukatsu), his name as a scholar was Silk Mountain (Razan), and his posthumous title was Versatile Writer. Master Razan was a person with extensive knowledge and a remarkable memory. He had particularly outstanding literary talent. He wrote continuously, and bequeathed a great number of books. Just to mention the most important, there are:

"Summary of the Eastern Mirror"『東鑑綱要』(*Azumakagami kōyō*)

"Complement to the *Essential Politics of the Documents*"『群書治要補』

"Records of Critical Reflections on Confucianism"『儒門思問録』

"The Legal Systems of Japan and China"『倭漢法制』

"Chronological Records of Our Dynasty"『本朝編年録』

"Compendium of the *Essentials of Upright View [Era] Politics*"『貞觀政要抄』(*Jōgan sei yōshō*)

"Examination of the Armillary Sphere"『渾天儀考』

"Commentary to the *Terminology of Nature and Principle*"『性理字義諺解』

"Examination of the Classics in Japanese"『經籍和字考』(*Keiseki waji kō*)

"Compendium of the *Four Books' Collected Commentaries*" 『四書集註抄』 (*Shisho shitchū shō*)
"Short Narrative of the Transmission of the Path" 『道統小傳』
"The Secret Transmission of Shinto" 『神道秘傳』
"Investigating the Shrines of Our Country" 『本朝神社考』

During his lifetime, he wrote or compiled a total of more than 170 works. The letters of Master Razan fill more than 150 fascicles. He was, indeed, a great writer and erudite of early modern times. Since his demise, the learning of the Hayashi family has been transmitted until today. It dominated the two hundred and fifty years of Tokugawa rule. Since it was through him that the learning of the literati was greatly invigorated, the Master can truly be called the Restorer of Confucianism.

FURTHER READING. An article in the *Encyclopedia of Confucianism* (ed. XINZHONG Y., Routledge, 2003) provides an informative and critical outline of HAYASHI Razan's biography. The most detailed account of Razan's Confucian thought in English is the study, *Adoption and Adaption of Neo-Confucianism in Japan: The Role of Fujiwara Seika and Hayashi Razan* by W. J. BOOT (3rd. rev. ed., 2013). What was originally Boot's dissertation can be found online—together with other source materials revolving around Razan's work, *Investigating Our Country's Shrines*—on the homepage of the Netherlands Association for Japanese Studies (ngjs.nl). The *Sources of Japanese Tradition* (ed. W. T. de BARY et al., 2nd. ed., Columbia UP, 2002, vol. 2, pt. 1), and the sourcebook, *Japanese Philosophy* (ed. J. W. HEISIG et al., Hawaii UP, 2011), each contain about fifteen pages of translations from several works by Razan.

本朝神社考

Gyonen

釋凝然
藤原　高橋
伊予
示観

The honorable Shaku Gyōnen (1240–1321) was born into the Wisteriafield (Fujiwara) clan of Highbridge (Takahashi) County, in Iyo province, more than 700 years ago, in 1240. His Buddhist name is Pointer to Insight (Jikan). He was naturally bright, and he had a deep connection to Buddhism. Since his childhood days he enjoyed hearing Buddhist teachings. Everything he was taught by anyone—at any time—he memorized and never forgot.

戒壇院
東大寺　奈良
圓照
華嚴
三論
禪學
後宇多

At the age of only fifteen years, he joined the Ordination Platform Convent of the Great Temple of the East (Tōdai-ji), in Nara. He shaved his head and took the precepts under the guidance of the priest Full Illumination (Enshō). Following that, he learned from a sectarian scholar Flower Ornament (Ch. Huáyán, Jp. Kegon) thought. Thereafter, he was also trained in the various teachings of the Yogācāra and Three Treatise schools. On a pilgrimage to Kyoto, he further grasped the principles of Zen-Learning. Parallelly, he also delved into the ways of Lǎozǐ and Zhuāngzǐ as well as those of the Hundred Philosophers. Although he was of such pervasive learning and ample knowledge that he awakened to the unity of the various sectarian doctrines, he himself took Flower Ornament studies as his true field. When he first lectured in the Great Buddha Hall, all of the teachers of the Seven Great Temples of the Southern Capital (i.e., Nara) rushed there to attend. Thereafter, an audience assembled like clouds every time he was lecturing. When Emperor Multiple Firmament (the Latter) (Gouda), made a pilgrimage to the Southern Capital, Gyōnen had the honor of bestowing upon him the Bodhisattva precepts. According to his biography, he was then formally asked to lecture about the *Treatise on the Five Teachings*, and was given the title of National Teacher. He entered *nirvāṇa* in the Ordination Platform Convent in 1321, on day five of the ninth month, and was buried on Hawk Tail Mountain (Mt. Takao). He was 81 years old and had lived for 66 years as a monk.

五教章

鷹尾山

His learning encompassed various doctrines and diverse sects. He delved into various subjects in Japanese and Chinese. And although he personally regarded Flower Ornament Buddhism as his home sect, he had no biases or prejudices. The greatest among his works are, "Thread into Depth and Darkness of the *Records in Pursuit of the Profundities of the Flower Ornament*" (120 fascicles) and "Pathway Records of the *Treatise on the Five Teachings*" (52 fascicles). Among the most widely circulated are, the "Essentials of the Eight Sects" and "Circumstances of the Spread of Buddhism through the Three Countries."

華嚴探玄記洞幽紗

五教章通路記

八宗綱要

三國佛法傳通縁起

However, here is not the place to list his works one by one. Over his lifetime he published more than 1,100 fascicles, in more than 160 volumes. Wasn't he a truly astonishing writer? Without writing any draft or making any corrections, he took the brush, wrote down thousand or ten thousand words, and finished an extensive masterpiece in less than a day. He was truly a genius rarely seen in the world, and moreover a man of accomplished great virtue.

Further Reading. There are short articles about Gyōnen in the *Digital Dictionary of Buddhism* (ed. A. C. Muller, buddhism-dict.net), and in the *Encyclopedia of Buddhism* (ed. R. E. Buswell, Macmillan, 2003). The article in the latter reference is written by Mark L. Blum, whose monograph presents a study and a translation of a work

浄土法門源流章

by Gyōnen called *Jōdo hōmon genru shō*. The translated title, namely *The Origins and Development of Pure Land Buddhism* (Oxford UP, 2002), was also used by BLUM as the title for his book. BLUM's study also contains a substantial chapter about "The Life and Thought of Gyōnen," as well as a bibliography of extant works. According to BLUM's research, the number of Gyōnen's writings given by Enryō, i.e., "more than 1,100 fascicles, in more than 160 volumes" could actually be realistic.

Afterword by Inoue Genichi (1965)

I add here a story about Prof. Dr. NITOBE Inazō, a famous Japanese diplomat and former principal of the First High School. At the beginning of an extension lecture for us students, who were great in number, I remember that he cited Thomas CARLYLE's words, "I am alone with the stars." Prof. Inazō told us that the Scottish author's study was under a glass ceiling roof, through which he could stare at the glimmering stars. During his lecture, the professor quoted the philosopher Diogenes Teufelsdröckh, the hero of Carlyle's novel, *Sartor Resartus* (1831):

新渡戸稲造

> O Nature!—Or what is Nature? Ha! why do I not name thee God? Art not thou the 'Living Garment of God?' O Heavens, is it, in very deed, He, then, that ever speaks through thee; that lives and loves in thee, that lives and loves in me? [...] Love not Pleasure; love God. This is the Everlasting Yea, wherein all contradiction is solved: Wherein whose walks and works, it is well with him. [...] Most true is it, as a wise man teaches us, that 'Doubt of any sort cannot be removed except by Action.'

The mental stages of Carlyle's hero, which led him from the "Everlasting No" over the "Center of Indifference" to the "Everlasting Yea," are different from Christianity, and rather conform with Oriental philosophy. The transformation from thought to action at least resonates well with my father's Philosophical Religion.

I mentioned in the introduction that the philosophy of Enryō in his later life might be different from modern philosophy. In the early Enlightened Rule (Meiji) era,

明治

philosophy—which Enryō cherished so much—dominated all academic study. But Enryō eventually found that our scholars had embraced the doctrines of Occidental scholars and tried to explain them to the people without initiative and originality. Unsympathetic to such slavish acceptance of ideas, he decided to live his life in his own way (as he had done for the preceding fifty years), and he realized that it was his mission to better the world by popularizing the sublime truths of philosophy as well as by developing its practical aspects.[50]

The present conditions of Japan seem particularly appropriate to study the significance of the Temple Garden of Philosophy. From my perspective as the one most familiar with Enryō himself, his thoughts seem to appear vividly in his arrangement of the Garden. His transcendent states of mind touch my heart through his sublime fidelity. This philosophic tone itself transforms this immortal Temple, but among thousands of visitors, few may leave with real understanding of its meaning.

This pamphlet is a partly rewritten translation of mine, which was originally completed nearly forty years ago with the help of American authorities. It was my turn to revise it in broken English, and thus the style of English may appear inconsistent at times. I have been sick in bed for a couple of weeks recently, and have lost my memory—especially of the English language. So, however awkward my words may be, I hope the reader will kindly excuse me for introducing a piece of my life's work to some friends.

50 Genichi notes: This and following paragraphs were written with the help of Dr. Sc. IKEHARA Shikao 池原止戈夫 (Tokyo Institute of Technology, Department of Mathematics), and his nephew MUTŌ Akira 武藤章, both of whom I was with on board a steamer to America in 1921.

APPENDIX

A. The 77 Features of the Temple Garden of Philosophy

No.	Feature	Reading	Trans. Genichi	Trans. Schulzer	Chap.	Remark
①	哲學關	*Tetsugaku kan*	Portcullis of Philosophy	Gateway to Philosophy	2	
②	眞理界	*Shinri kai*	Sphere of Truth	Realm of Truth	2	
③	讃仰軒	*Sangyō ken*		House of Praise	2	
④	哲理門	*Tetsuri mon*	Portal of Metaphysics	Gate of Philosophical Reason	2, 17	
⑤	一元牆	*Ichigen shō*		Hedge of Monism	2	
⑥	常識門	*Jōshiki mon*	Gate of Common Sense	Gate of Common Sense	2	
⑦	髑髏庵	*Dokuro an*	Hut of the Skull	Skull Hermitage	3	
⑧	復活廊	*Fukkatsu rō*		Corridor of Resurrection	3	
⑨	鬼神窟	*Kishin kutsu*	House of the Gods	Hollow of Gods and Spirits	3	
⑩	接神室	*Sesshin shitsu*		Chamber to Touch the Divine	3	
⑪	靈明閣	*Reimei kaku*		Loft of Spiritual Light	3	
⑫	天狗松	*Tengu matsu*	Tengu Pine	Kobold Pine	3	cf. 70
⑬	時空岡	*Jikū kō*	Hill of Time and Space	Hill of Time and Space	4	
⑭	百科叢	*Hyakka sō*		Thicket of One Hundred Subjects	4	
⑮	四聖堂	*Shisei dō*	Shrine of the Four Sages	Four Sages Hall	4–7	
⑯	唱念塔	*Shōnen tō*	Mantra Pillar	Stele of Invocation	7	
⑰	六賢臺	*Rokken dai*	Pagoda of the Six Wise Men	Pagoda of the Six Wise Ones	8	
⑱	筆塚	*Fude zuka*	Brush-shaped Tomb	Brush Tomb	9	cf. 18

No.	Feature	Reading	Trans. Genichi	Trans. Schulzer	Chap.	Remark
⑲	懷疑巷	*Kaigi kō*	Crossroads of Skepticism	Fork of Doubt	9	
⑳	經驗坂	*Keiken zaka*	Slope of Experience	Slope of Experience	9	
㉑	感覺巒	*Kankaku ran*	Mound of the Sensation	Peak of Perception	9	
㉒	萬有林	*Banyū rin*	Universal Forest	Grove of Endless Beings	9	
㉓	三祖苑	*Sanso en*		Three Founders Yard	9	
㉔	三字壇	*Sanji dan*		三-shaped Podium, Tripartite Podium	9	
㉕	三祖碑	*Sanso hi*	Three Fathers Monument	Monument of the Three Founders	9	
㉖	哲史蹊	*Tesshi kei*	Route of Philosophical History	History of Philosophy Path	9	
㉗	唯物園	*Yuibutsu en*	Garden of Materialism	Garden of Materialism	10	cf. 47
㉘	物字壇	*Butsuji dan*		物-shaped Patch, Matter Patch	10	cf. 48
㉙	客觀廬	*Kyakkan ro*	Pavilion of Objectivity	Shelter of Objectivity	10	cf. 55
㉚	進化溝	*Shinka kō*	Furrow of Evolution	Canal of Evolution	10	
㉛	理化潭	*Rika tan*	Physico-Chemical Bay	Pool of Science	10	
㉜	博物隄	*Hakubutsu tei*	Bank of Biology	Weir of Natural History	10	
㉝	數理江	*Suiri kō*	Brook of Mathematics	River of Mathematics	10	
㉞	觀象梁	*Kanshō ryō*	Bridge of Phenomena	Observation Overpass	10	
㉟	望遠橋	*Bōen kyō*	Bridge of the Telescope	Telescope Catwalk	10	lost
㊱	星界洲	*Seikai su*	Starry Land	Land of Stars	10	
㊲	半月臺	*Hangetsu dai*	Crescent-shaped Balcony	Crescent Moon Balcony	10	lost

No.	Feature	Reading	Trans. Genichi	Trans. Schulzer	Chap.	Remark
㊳	神祕洞	*Shinpi dō*	Grotto of Mysticism	Cave of Mystery	10	
㊴	狸燈	*Ri tō*	Badger Lantern	Tanuki Lamp	10	cf. 52
㊵	後天沼	*Kōten numa*	A Posteriori Pool	Swamp of the A Posteriori	10	-*shō* [?]
㊶	原子橋	*Genshi kyō*	Bridge of the Atom	Bridge of the Atoms	10	
㊷	自然井	*Shizen sei*	Nature's Spring	Nature's Fountain	10	
㊸	造化澗	*Zōka kan*	Hollow of Creation	Ravine of Creation	11	
㊹	二元衢	*Nigen ku*	Junction of Dualism	Fork of Dualism	11	
㊺	學界津	*Gakkai tsu*	Inlet of Learning	Harbor of Academia	11	
㊻	獨斷峽	*Dokudan kyō*	Chasm of Dogmatism	Gorge of Dogma	11	
㊼	唯心庭	*Yuishin tei*	Garden of Idealism	Garden of Idealism	12	cf. 27
㊽	心字池	*Shinji ike*	Heart-shaped Pond	心-shaped Pond, Mind Pond	12	cf. 28
㊾	倫理淵	*Rinri en*	Stream of Ethics	Depths of Ethics	12	
㊿	心理崖	*Shinri gai*	Cliff of Psychology	Slope of Psychology	12	
51	理性島	*Risei jima*	Isle of Reason	Island of Reason	12	-*tō* [?]
52	鬼燈	*Ki tō*	Demon Lantern	Demon Lamp	12	cf. 39
53	概念橋	*Gainen kyō*	Bridge of Conception	Bridge of Concepts	12	
54	先天泉	*Senten sen*	A Priori Spring	Spring of the A Priori	12	
55	主觀亭	*Shukan tei*	Pavilion of Subjectivity	Pavilion of Subjectivity	12	cf. 29
56	直覺徑	*Chokkaku kei*	Path of Intuition	Shortcut of Intuition	13	
57	認識路	*Ninshiki ro*	Route of Cognition	Road of Cognition	13	
58	論理域	*Ronri iki*	Court of Logic	Domain of Logic	13	

No.	Feature	Reading	Trans. Genichi	Trans. Schulzer	Chap.	Remark
⑲	演繹觀	*En'eki kan*	Observatory of Deduction	View of Deduction	13	
⑳	歸納場	*Kinō jō*	Spot of Induction	Spot of Induction	13	
㉑	意識驛	*Ishiki eki*		Station of Consciousness	14	
㉒	絶對城	*Zettai jō*	Castle of the Absolute	Citadel of the Absolute	14	
㉓	聖哲碑	*Seitetsu hi*		Monument of the Sages	14	
㉔	觀念脚	*Kannen kyaku*		Gallery of Ideas	14	
㉕	觀察境	*Kansatsu kyō*		Realm of Contemplation	14	
㉖	紀念碑	*Kinen hi*		Enthronement Memorial Stone	14	
㉗	相對溪	*Sōtai kei*		Trench of the Relative	15	
㉘	理想橋	*Risō kyō*	Bridge of Ideals	Bridge of the Ideal	15	
㉙	理外門	*Rigai mon*	Gate of Tran-scendental Reason	Gate of the Transrational	15	
㉚	幽靈梅	*Yūrei bai*	Yurei Plum	Ghost Apricot	15	cf. 12
㉛	宇宙館	*Uchū kan*	Universe Hall	Cosmos Hall	16	
㉜	皇國殿	*Kōkoku den*	Imperial Forum	Imperial Dais	16	
㉝	三學亭	*Sangaku tei*	Pyramid of the Three Scholars	Three Erudites Arbor	17	
㉞	硯塚	*Suzuri zuka*		Inkstone Tomb	17	cf. 18
㉟	無盡藏	*Mujin zō*	Inexhaustible Treasure Land	Inexhaustible Treasury	17	
㊱	向上樓	*Kōjō rō*		Edifice of Elevation	17	
㊲	萬象庫	*Banshō ko*		Storehouse of Myriad Phenomena	17	

B. The Portrait of the Four Sages (1885)

四聖像
渡邊文三郎
哲學祭
中村正直
橋本雅邦
哲學堂祭

The Portrait of the Four Sages is an artwork by WATANABE Bunsaburō, that was created, at Enryō's request, for the first Philosophy Ceremony in 1885, presumably held on the campus of Tokyo University. The caption reproduced with translation below was composed by NAKAMURA Masanao, Enryō's university teacher of the Chinese classics.[51] Some years later, Enryō asked the artist HASHIMOTO Gahō to paint another picture of the Four Sages, which was finished in 1895, but never received a caption (TANAKA 2018). The picture scroll shown during today's Philosophy Shrine Ceremony held every year on a Sunday in the first half of November is a replica of the artwork by WATANABE Bunsaburō, which is still owned by the Inoue family.

文學士井上君使畫工作四聖像索余賛	Master of Literature Mr. Inoue requested the artist to paint the Portrait of the Four Sages and asked me to write the caption.
四聖者孔釋二氏及瑣克刺韓圖也	The Four Sages are Confucius, Buddha, Socrates, and Kant.

孔釋之教拯溺救焚	*The teachings of Confucius and Buddha:* *save them from drowning, rescue them from burning.*
若微二聖人禽奚分	*Were these two sages to vanish,* *how to distinguish humans from beasts!*

51 The English translation was possible with the kind help of Dr. TSUJII Yoshiteru 辻井義輝 and Prof. Timothy NEWFIELDS.

FIGURE 20. Portrait of the Four Sages by Watanabe Bunsaburō

歐州之哲尤推瑣韓	*Amongst the philosophers of Europe,* *Socrates and Kant are most upheld.*
知大宗師固道德根	*Knowing the teachers of the great traditions* *fastens the root of virtue.*
弱肉強食今尚不已	*The flesh of the weak is the fodder for the strong,* *Yet ever to this day.*
卓美之世何旹可待	*Ideal world of beauty:* *when can we foresee?*
炳燭餘光嗟我老矣	*Candlelight's remaining flare –* *ah! I've grown old.*
繼往開来望在俊士	*Following the past into an open future,* *hoping for men of excellence.*

明治乙酉十二月	December, Year Eighteen of Enlightenment Politics [1885]
正五位中村正直	[Court] Official of the Fifth Rank Nakamura Masanao

C. The Eight Views around the Philosophy Shrine

Inoue Enryō selected Eight Views around the Philosophy Shrine as being the chief scenes of natural beauty in the environment of his Garden:

哲學堂八景

1. 富士暮雪 *Twilight Snow on the Prosperous Lord*
2. 御霊帰鴉 *Homeward Flight of Crows to the Spirits Shrine*
3. 玉橋秋月 *Autumnal Moon over the Crystal Bridge*
4. 氷川夕照 *Sunset Glow over Frozen River Lowland*
5. 薬師晩鐘 *Evening Bell of the Healing Temple*
6. 古田落雁 *Wild Geese Alighting upon the Old Paddies*
7. 鼓岡晴嵐 *Azure Skies over the Windswept Drum Hill*
8. 魔松夜雨 *Night Rain Enshrouding the Demon Pine*

Although the concept of distinguishing eight eminent views stems from China, Enryō closely followed the Japanese example of the Eight Views of Close Waters (*Ōmi hakkei*).[52]

近江八景

The eight views described by Enryō in 1904 are, however, entirely different from the present environment. At that time, the Temple Garden of Philosophy stood in a lonely village in the Warrior Hide Plain (Musashino).[53] Now a residential area of the Eastern Capital (i.e., Tokyo), such scenes are not found anywhere in the surroundings. However, from Enryō's descriptions, old photographs and maps it is possible to reconstruct the meaning of Enryo's Eight Views (Maejima 1980, Ideno 2011). Genichi's translation and comments as well as the drawing reproduced below further help to imagine the scenery.

武藏野

52 Ideno 2011. The characters 近江, here literally translated as "close waters," are an old name for the Lute Lake 琵琶湖 (i.e., Lake Biwa). Phonetically, *ōmi* has a different etymology meaning "fresh water."

53 Phonetic etymology of *musashi* is obscure.

FIGURE 21. Chart of the Eight Views around the Philosophy Shrine

石本秋園

The "Chart of the Eight Views around the Philosophy Shrine" (fig. 21) was drawn by ISHIMOTO Shūen in 1904. The drawing, which shows the Philosophy Shrine from the north-eastern direction, names ten places. Most of the names appear in Genichi's explanations of the Eight Views given below.

From left to right, the places shown in figure 21 are,

御靈社	Venerable Spirits Shrine (*Goryō-sha*)
玉橋	Chrystal Bridge
新井藥師	Medicine Buddha in New Wells (*Arai Yakushi*)
鼓罡	Drum Hill (*Tsuzumi-ga-oka*)
古田	Old Paddies
葛ヶ谷	Vine Valley (*Kuzu-ga-yato*)
片山	One-sided Mountain
魔松	Demon Pine
小学校	Elementary School
氷川社	Frozen River Shrine
東村	Eastern Village

FIGURE 22. Northern view of the Temple Garden of Philosophy, 1914

The Eight Views around the Philosophy Shrine

1. Twilight Snow on the Prosperous Lord

On a clear day, Mount Prosperous Lord 富士山 (Mt. Fuji)[54] can be seen from the ⑬ Hill of Time and Space. As evening approaches, the beauty of this view is greatly enhanced by the translucent hues of the sky.

2. Homeward Flight of Crows to the Spirits Shrine

The Venerable Spirits Shrine 御靈神社 (*Goryō-jinja*) is a small village sanctuary, consecrated to Prince Yamato-takeru, a mythological hero of ancient times. The Shrine, which is in the midst of a cedar grove, is located a stone's throw from the Temple Garden. [55]

3. Autumnal Moon over the Crystal Bridge

The Crystal Bridge is found to the southeast of the Garden of Idealism; it is built across the Temple River of Wondrous Uprightness

54 Phonetic etymology of *fuji* is obscure.

55 Genichi notes: There was a large bamboo field near the shrine.

妙正寺川 (*Myōshō-ji-gawa*) that takes its course along the boundary of the Garden. [56]

4. Sunset Glow over Frozen River Lowland

Frozen River 氷川 (*Hikawa*) Lowland lies to the northwest of the Garden. It presents a most beautiful picture at sunset, the glow covering the Frozen River Shrine 氷川神社, the tutelary shrine of Old Paddy Waters 江古田 (*Ekoda*).

5. Evening Bell of the Healing Temple

The Apricot Gloss Temple 梅照院 (*Baishō-in*) consecrated to Yakushi 薬師, the Healing or Medicine Buddha, may be passed on the way from Midfield to the Temple Garden. The sound of its bell floating out upon the evening air lends peace and serenity to the landscape all around.

6. Wild Geese Alighting upon the Old Paddies

The rice fields on the other side of the brook of Old Paddy Waters attract the wild geese that flock to this spot in great number. [57]

7. Azure Skies over the Windswept Drum Hill

Under a clear autumnal sky, gales sweep over the wooded slopes of the Drum Hill 鼓岡 (*Tsuzumi-ga-oka*), which lies beyond the Temple River of Wondrous Uprightness opposite of Peaceful Paddy Hill 和田山 (*Wadayama*), the hill of the Temple Garden of Philosophy. [58]

56 Visitors who take the Midfield 中野 (Nakano) or the Eastern Midfield route will pass over this bridge, the common name of which is the Four Villages Bridge 四村橋 (*Shimura-bashi*).

57 Genichi notes: I recollect a watermill in the neighboring land between our apricot garden and Old Paddy Waters 江古田, which added a touch of ruralness to the scene.

58 Genichi notes: The Drum Hill had been covered with oak bushes and a thick forest of cedars. Attacked by air raids, the forest and bushes were burnt during the war.

8. Night Rain Enshrouding the Demon Pine

The soft rain pattering upon the tree, in the dead of night, enhances the mysticism in the atmosphere all around. The mystic tree mentioned here is the ⑫ Kobold Pine.

D. Hermit Life (c. 1915–1919)

絶句

律詩

仙居

The following is an adaption by Charlotte Frietch of verses by Enryō collected in source J.4 (1920) (see Editorial Notes). The stanzas are composed in three different classical forms of Chinese poetry. The first three stanzas which Enryō composed in 1915 (IS 14: 226–27) are "quatrains" of seven characters each (I.–III.). They are followed by five "regulated verses" with eight lines of five characters each (IV.–VIII.). The poem ends with one regulated verse with eight lines of seven characters each (IX.) (Ideno 2011: 133). The dates of origin of the stanzas IV to IX is unknown, and it is uncertain whether they were printed during Enryō's lifetime. It is also questionable whether the verses as they appear below were intended by Enryō to constitute a single poem and whether the title originates from him. The Japanese title *Sen'i* does not appear in source J.4 (1920), but is mentioned by Genichi in J.6.

I.

清風一過萬松鳴
自作唯心唯物聲
聽到門前有知巴
幽靈天狗笑相迎

A blast of pure wind —
A thousand pine needles rustle,
Rousing the voices of Matter and Spirit.
I hear these voices;
I go to the gate and find —
Friends familiar, Kobold and Ghost.
Smiling, they welcome me.

II.

哲學堂成已十秋
友賢師聖復何求
一筆疎食吾生足
身不自由心自由

Accomplished is the task of building
The Temple of Philosophy!
Since then, ten autumns have come and fled.
As instructors, I count saints;
Naught else is there that I do crave!
Simple fare my flesh desires, — yoked it is to matter;

The spirit freed will soar on high to Empyrean bliss!

III. 哲學堂前過者誰
出門相見是吾師
囊無一物難賖酒
笑使幽靈陳謝辭

Who is this shadow loitering before the Temple gate?
I approach the gate and gaze upon the shadow.
My tutor 'tis of bygone days, I see,
Naught, alas in my purse have I!
Wherewith to buy my friend a sip of wine!
Let the statue of the Ghost, grin and proffer an excuse!

IV. 野方村盡處
丘上設仙莊
天狗松陰路
幽靈梅畔堂
汲泉朝煮茗
掃席晩焚香
入夜裁詩句
閑中自有忙

On the Bounds of the village Fieldside
upon the hill, a hermitage I built.
The shadows of the Kobold fall upon the routes;
Near the Ghost Apricot the Temple stands.
In the early morn I take water
from the spring, —
And then I brew myself a cup of tea
As dusk draws nigh, I put my house in order,
And then the smoke of incense curls on high.
In the dark of night I make my poems,
Leisure moments have I, yet, — the hours of life are crowded!

V. 無客門常鎖
菜畦路稍通
洗心玉溪水
養氣鼓岡風
醉處吾忘我
吟邊色即空
俗塵渾不到
靜坐守仙宮

Guestless; hence I close my door,
Upon the fields of verdant green
Where a narrow path, but one, is trodden,
I cleanse my mind in the jeweled crystal brook;
I feast my spirit on the Drum-hill breeze;
I sip of heavenly nectar — and oblivion's mine.
Into the land of verse I delve
Matter is a hollow nothing!
Away I flee from the worldly dust!
Silent I sit; a sentinel
Watchfully guarding the hermitage.

VI. 聖堂深處坐
兀々似禪僧
守默疲凭几
讀書倦曲肱
屈伸身自在
迷悟意全能
終日無塵累
我居是武陵

In the inner sanctuary of the holy hall,
Like a lone musing priest am I,
Silent and weary I lean on my desk;
Tired I am of reading my books!
I rest my head in the curve of my arm.
As it lists, my body relaxes
enchanted, or freed, my spirit works at will, —
Never is it yoked to worldly matters!
An eternal Hermit's Land of Dreams, —
Is this abode of mine!

VII. 體髏庵獨坐
詩書作良媒
雖設門常鎖
不招客自來
雨聲涵瘦竹
月影宿疎梅
醉後漫敲句
呼童掃硯埃

Alone I sit within the "Hut of Skulls"!
A book of verse companies me;
A gate there is, but ever chained;
We beckon none, yet guests do come!
Down the slender, shining bamboo trunks,
The gently dripping raindrops patter
The silvering shadows of the moon,
The barren apricot embraces.
Enchanted by the spirit wine,
Freely will the verses flow;
I bid the servant my equipment to prepare,
For my Muse is waiting at the door.

VIII. 天國繞吾屋
六塵悉福音
開雷知夏到
見雪覺冬深
秋月浮禪味
春花映道心
四時佳興足
朝夕枕肱吟

Atmosphere celestial dwells around my house!
Heavenly are the sounds of all mundane things!
I hear Thunder tell me summer is near, —
Snow I see, and know now winter's at its height;
From the autumn moon, the tones of Transcendentalism flow;
Blossoms of the spring, the hermit's mind reflects;
Seasons all are full of happiness!
Morning, noon, and night,
I chant, my head upon my arm!

IX. 哲學堂深世事疎
清閑最好閲仙書
風青天狗松陰路
月白幽靈梅畔廬
欲究六塵悉文字
靜觀萬法即眞如
更鞭理想遊方外
踞物繙心讀大虚

In the inner circle doth the Temple lie,
Distant from all worldly matter,
Pure the atmosphere, and tranquil;
Fit it is to dwell with books of mystic realms!
Winds of blue are blowing —
On the route the Kobold Pine is shading!
White the moon is shining —
On the hut the Ghost Apricot the light's reflecting!
Mundane things I wish to study;
Hence, I trace the records made by man.
Into my Self I gaze to find: The universe is One.[59]
Onward is the steed Ideal spurred —
Into a sphere beyond the world!
In the midst of things material,
I, the book of Spirit open,
There to find Eternity!

59 Genichi felt that the Buddhist resonance of line five and six of the last stanza got lost in the translation. Therefore, he proposed to translate, "World of phenomena I seek to explore, From whence I trace all Words and Sounds. Into my Self I gaze to find, The Universe is itself the Absolute Truth" (Source E.3). Even more literally, the phrase in question 萬法即真如 can be translated "the myriad phenomena are but suchness." The East Asian Buddhist notion that the phenomenal world is itself the ultimate truth was reformulated in modern terms by Inoue Tetsujirō 井上哲次郎 (1856–1944) as "phenomena-sive-being theory" 現象即實在論, or Identity Realism. This philosophy is often considered the first original Japanese philosophy of the modern era.

E. Extract from "My Mission in Philosophy" (1919)

The following is an abstract, made by INOUE Genichi, of what is one of Enryō's last published writings (Source J.3). The article is significant as a programmatic statement of what Enryō planned to achieve with the Temple Garden of Philosophy. A complete translation of "My Philosophical Mission," by Dylan Luers TODA, is published in volume three of *International Inoue Enryo Research* (2015).

哲學上に於ける余の使命

(1) What is the Temple Garden of Philosophy?

I beg the reader to bear in mind that the Temple Garden of Philosophy on Peaceful Paddy Hill is an institute for social education—a center for the Realization of Philosophy 哲學の實行化. I call it the Philosophy Temple on Mount Morality 哲學寺道徳山.

(2) What is the Realization of Philosophy?

I have been engaged in the task of the Realization of Philosophy, that is, the practice of philosophy for the benefit of public welfare. The philosophy of the West inclines towards reason alone, and considers the practical side of philosophy to be negligible. It possesses sight, but no limbs. I believe that the ultimate object of philosophy lies in its practical application. From within the confines of the transcendental abstract spheres of philosophy, I am striving to open a route that would lead to practical application.

(3) What is the Philosophical Religion?

The religion expressed in this Temple differs from the idea of religion according to the common use of the word. It is rather a philosophy. In other words, philosophical belief is based on reason, and not on mere religious sentiment. Buddhism is a philosophical religion, as we know, and therefore it is in accord with my own philosophical religion. The main difference between the two is that Buddhism is founded on the individual character of Śākyamuni Buddha.

(4) What is the Relation between Faith and Reason?

I may say that, on the one hand, I believe in a philosophical religion, and on the other hand, in the True Pure Land School of Buddhism 淨土眞宗. As I was born in a pious True School family, the seeds of the True School naturally appear before my mind's eye. There may be those who contend that one cannot hold two faiths. But I maintain that there are two forms of belief. Just as we have intellect and feeling within ourselves, there are two aspects of belief. And although the two appear to be separate, the principal body of belief is nevertheless one; hence, an individual system of belief can display itself as a philosophical religion when viewed from one side, and take the form of the True School teachings when seen from the other. Moreover, the back view is not limited to the True School teachings alone, for sometimes it might appear in the form of the Zen School 禪宗, or the other sects, all according to the individual viewpoint.

F. Brief History of the Garden

哲学堂公園の由来
中野区

On the avenue leading from the road at the east side of the park, half way to the entrance of the Garden, there stands on the right hand side a metal information board. The board, which gives concise information about the "Origin of the Temple Garden of Philosophy," was placed there by Midfield City (Nakano-ku), probably in 1975. Genichi bequeathed an English translation of an information board that used to be on that very spot. However, that translation cannot be based on the present board because the translation dates from the year 1959. When comparing the Japanese text of the present board with Genichi's 1959 translation, it becomes clear that Midfield City reproduced most of the text from the preceding board, only omitting the second and adding a last paragraph. Below, I supplemented the translation of the last paragraph.

哲学堂は、東洋大学の創立者である故井上円了先生が国家社会の恩に報いるために、護国愛理の理想に基づき国民道徳の普及を目的として、明治三十九年以来私財を投じ、自ら堂主となって独力経営された精神修養的公園であります。	The Temple Garden of Philosophy is a park for mental cultivation that was managed by the founder, Inoue Enryō, Lit. D. Based on the ideals of Protection of Country and Love of Truth, it was established in the Year 39 of the Enlightened Rule (Meiji) era [1906], by contributions of his own funds, in filial gratitude for the benefits he received from his country and society.
[not on the present board]	The garden is pervaded by the atmosphere of the Warrior Hide Plain 武藏野, and it is abundant with historical facts and traditions (e.g., Peaceful Paddy Hill 和田山 is believed to have been the mansion of Wada Yoshimori 和田義

盛 during the Scythe Storehouse 鎌倉 (Kamakura) period, 1185–1333).

園地は、先生が唱えられた実践哲学の理像を表わす多くの施設と特異な造園手法とを加えて、都下の名所として人々に親しまれてきました。

The peculiar garden techniques, and the many buildings based on Dr. Inoue's ideals of practical philosophy, make the garden a famous place among the people in the Tokyo suburb.

大正八年六月、先生は大陸巡遊の途中大連の宿舎でなくなられましたので、嗣子故井上玄一氏は、その志を続いで本園を経営すること二十余年に及びましたが、昭和十九年三月、公益優先の趣旨に則り、この園地一切を挙げて東京都に寄付されました。

In June, Year 8 of the Great Justice (Taishō) era [1919], when Dr. Inoue was on his lecturing tour in China, he died suddenly in Dàlián. In accordance with Enryō's will and testament, Mr. Inoue Genichi, Enryō's eldest son and heir, took office as manager of the Temple Garden for about twenty years. In March, Year 19 of the Shining Harmony (Shōwa) era [1944], he donated the shrine, the buildings, and most of the estate to the Tokyo Municipality in the interest of public benefit.

東京都では、故人の遺志を尊重し管理することになり、全国にもまれな文化修養公園として公開してきました。

Respecting its founder's will, it was decided to open the park to the public as a garden for civilization and culture unique to the nation.

昭和五十年四月一日、中野区は東京都から移管を受け、歴史性の深い文化財公園、又区民の緑のオアシスとして公開しております。

On April 1, Year 51 of the Shining Harmony era [1975], the administration of the park was transferred from Tokyo Municipality to Midfield City. As a park of high cultural and historical value, and as a green oasis for the residents, we open it to the public.

G. The Tomb of Inoue Enryo

井上圓了
井上敬
蓮華寺

The tomb of Inoue Enryō (1858–1919), and his wife, Inoue Kei (1862–1951), lies in the cemetery of the Buddhist Lotus Flower Temple (Renge-ji), which is adjacent to the grounds of the Temple Garden of Philosophy, about one hundred meters northwest of the Garden's main entrance. Inoue Kei was born 1862, and died on January 4, 1951, at the age of 90 (according to pre-modern Japanese age counting). She was buried next to her husband.

井 上 圓 了

The tombstone, made of granite, was designed by Inoue Enryō himself. The design is based on the four Chinese characters that make up Enryō's name. In Japanese order: the signify "well," "upon," "round," and "perfect." Literally translated, it means "round perfection upon the well."[60] His playfulness led Enryō to make use of this meaning for his tomb. The circular stone slab represents the "round perfection," and the quadrangular pedestal is in the form of the Chinese character for "well." He placed the slab upon the pedestal, thus symbolizing his full name. At either side of the tomb, two cypress trees—grown from seeds brought home by Enryō from the tomb of Confucius, near the town Bend Hill (Qūfù)—were planted. Unfortunately, both withered with time, and they were replaced by ordinary Japanese cypresses.

曲阜

井上圓了之墓
南條文雄

The characters engraved on the circular slab on the front side of Enryō's grave mean "Tomb of Inoue Enryō." The Chinese ideographs were engraved based on the calligraphy by Dr. Nanjō Bun'yū, a scholar of Buddhism and Sanskrit, who was Enryō's intimate friend. Another

60 The modern version of 圓 is 円. Today, Enryō's name is mostly written accordingly.

FIGURE 23. Tomb of Inoue Enryō

good friend of Enryō, Professor of Chinese Literature at Toyo University TSUCHIYA Hiroshi (pen-name: Phoenix Land), composed in May 1920 the "Dedication to Mr. Hosui Inoue's Spirit," which is engraved on the two outer sides of the tomb's pedestal.

土屋弘　鳳洲
甫水井上君靈表

君名圓了井上氏號甫
水安政五年二月四日
誕于越後三島郡浦村
考日圓悟妣大溪氏君
爲入魁偉心匠精密才
略超群明治十一年秋
入東京大學豫備門
十八年七月畢哲學
科業時齡二十八也
二十九年選爲博士

He was called Enryō; his surname was Inoue; Hosui was his pen-name. He was born on the 4th of February, 1858, in the Riverbank village in Three Island county of the ultramontane region. His father's name was Engo; the maiden name of his mother, Ōtani. Enryō was a great character, exquisite in mind, and incomparable in talent. He entered the Tokyo University Preparatory School in 1878, and graduated from the university's Philosophy Department in 1885, being 28 years of age. He was bestowed a doctorate in 1896.

方是時歐學欝興儒衰
慶君慨然歎白此因失
爲學之序首倡道東洋
學剏大學開中學射往
海外考覈學理

During these years, Western science was on the rise in Japan, while Confucianism and Buddhism were on the decline. Filled with sorrow, Inoue Enryō attributed it to a wrong method of learning. Hence he proclaimed it his mission to restore Oriental teaching. He erected a college and opened a high school. He made trips abroad to investigate research and education.

後購近郊野方村和田
山地一萬五于步建哲
學堂祀孔瑣韓四子又
設六賢臺三學亭自選
數十勝築圖書館財古
今內外書籍數萬卷君
畢生志業在於統合東
西學術精窮哲理調護
國體矣

In his later years, he bought about thirteen acres of ground on Peaceful Paddy Hill, in the suburban village Fieldside. On this plot of ground, he erected the Philosophy Shrine for the veneration of Confucius, Buddha, Socrates, and Kant. He built the Pagoda of the Six Wise Men, and the Three Erudites Arbor. He himself selected some seventy superb features [in the Garden], erected a library, and stored therein thousands upon thousands of ancient and modern books from home and abroad. His life's work was to bring together the scholarship of the East and the West, and to find the essence of philosophical truth [common to both]. Thus he would protect and perpetuate the national integrity.

其巡遊海內外講學宣
教爲是也其陶鑄俊髦
數千人著書一百餘種
亦爲是也

Inspired by this [lofty ideal], he undertook tours home and abroad, and delivered lectures and spread education. The same [noble purpose] led him to direct his efforts toward the education of thousands of superior minds and the writing of more than a hundred books.

大正八年五月巡歷支
那至大連一夕俄發病
遂不起実六月六日也
其二十二日窀穸遺骨
於和田山塋域享齡
六十二配吉田氏擧一
男二女男玄一嗣來囑

In May, 1919, he was touring China as he came to Dàlián, where he had an attack of apoplexy from which he did not recover. He died on June 6th, at the age of sixty-one. On June 22nd, his ashes were interred on the cemetery of Peaceful Paddy Hill. He left a widow, née Yoshida, one son, and two daughters. His son and heir, Genichi, requested

予文因述其平生梗概 授之以鐫貞珉頌日	me to write this inscription. Hence, I presented this short biography, which has been engraved on the tombstone together with the following Hymn:
國文漢書、梵典歐籍 兼修剖鑽、徵諸實歷 終生孜孜、墨突孔席 經營得宜、舉措厎績 緊如斯人、邦家柱石	He was an ardent student of National Literature, the Chinese Classics, the Indian Sūtras, as well as European Philosophy. He pursued these studies analytically, and tested them in real life. With the persistent zeal of Mòzǐ, and the untiring industry of Confucius, he gave his whole life to this noble work. His efficiency in management brought about extensive achievements. Alas! Such a man was he, a pillar of our country!

On the backside of the slab, the posthumous Buddhist title of Enryō is engraved next to the one of his wife Kei. The right side shows the calligraphy, *Hosui-in Shaku-Enryō*; the left side, *Hōden-in Shaku-Myōkei*. Seedling Water (Hosui) is Enryō's pen-name, and is derived from the two elements that make up the character that refers to his native village, Riverbank (Ura). The character which reads *in* is a Buddhist convent, and *shaku* refers to the Śākya clan of the historical Buddha. A literal translation of the title could read, "The Perfect One from the Riverbank Convent of the Śākya Clan." The first two characters of Kei's posthumous title *hōden* can be read in the same way as her maiden name, i.e., Yoshida. The character *hō*, which means "fragrance," further alludes to the second name of Kei's mother. Kei's posthumous Buddhist name therefore expresses, "The Wonderful Reverent One from the Fragrant Field Nunnery of the Śākya Clan."

甫水院釋圓了
芳田院釋妙敬
甫水

浦
院
釋

芳田
吉田　芳

Although Enryō liked to interpret his name as "full (or "round") perfection," the Buddhist names of his family suggest otherwise. His father was called Engo (Full

圓悟

圓解 圓實

Awakening). His uncle's name was Enkai (Full Comprehension), and Enryō's grandfather had the name Enjitsu (Full Verification). The idea of lineage that is expressed in the analogous naming of the successors is common in parishioner temples of the True Pure Land School of Buddhism. Accordingly, *ryō* in Enryō's name must be translated as "understanding," rather than "round." His complete name thus would have the meaning Full Understanding. However, Enryō declined to succeed his father as head priest of their family's temple. The name he gave to his son suggests that he had in mind to create a new lineage. In a draft of this guide (Source E.4), Genichi mentions that his name was chosen by Enryō "according to Laotse's *Sūtra on Morality*, that is, *gen* being one (*ichi*) road." Although the characters *gen-ichi* do not appear in the *Dàodéjīng* (Guideline to the path of virtue) in this combination, both characters appear prominently in section ten of the text which is traditionally ascribed to Lǎozǐ. A literal translation of Genichi's name therefore could be Mysterious Unity, resonating the notion of perfection in Enryō's own name.[61]

了 玄 一 道德經 老子

61 The correct transcription of 玄一 would be Gen'ichi. I omitted the apostrophe in the main text for style reasons.

Editorial Notes

The single most important source for understanding the Temple Garden of Philosophy is a guided tour of the park conducted by Inoue Enryō 井上圓了 (1858–1919), probably in 1915. The transcript of these oral explanations was first published in December, 1915, and thereafter revised and reprinted several times as "Guide to the Philosophy Shrine"『哲學堂案内』(see below J.4). Based on this Japanese guide, Enryō's son, Inoue Genichi 井上玄一 (1887–1972), worked to produce an English guidebook, which apparently never went into print. There exist, however, the following English language fragments, written by Genichi, that became the basis for this edition.

E.1 "Outlines of the Temple-Garden of Philosophy," photocopy of handwritten manuscript, 88 pages (date unknown). Chapters 1–4 (30 pages) missing. Chapters 14–17 unfinished. The text originates from Genichi's stay in the USA (1921–1925). Notes added and copied after 1945. Whereabouts of the original manuscript unknown. Photocopy held by Inoue Enryo Research Center.

E.2 「亡父の忌日に際して」[On the occasion of the anniversary of my father's death], including "Introduction to the English Edition" (1925) and "Preface" (1920),『觀想』[Contemplation] (extra number) 21 (1925): pp. 1–5+xi.

E.3 「哲学堂概説追録：英訳文例添付」[Supplement to the outline of the Philosophy Shrine: English translation samples attached], 7+ix pages (Dec. 1962). Additional printing as supplement to J.6 (see below). Original held by Inoue Enryo Research Center.

E.4 「哲学堂関係：井上玄一氏来信綴」[Collection of correspondence from Inoue Gen'ichi related to the Philosophy Shrine] (1963–1965). Collected by the addressee Yumoto Takeo [?] 湯本武雄.

Letters and postcards in Japanese, notes in English and Japanese, several type-written English drafts. Materials for an additional part with the title, "Glimpse of Tetsugakudo." Original held by Inoue Enryo Research Center.

Genichi began his work for the "internationalization" (see Introduction) of his father's late-life work during his stay in the United States of America from 1921 to 1925. Although Genichi apparently was able to produce a nearly finished draft by the time of his return, there is no extant printed version of it. Almost 40 years later, in preparation for the 1964 Tokyo Olympics, he made another attempt to publish an English guide. However, perhaps due to his age (by then 75), or due to the absence of sufficient help from an English native speaker, again no English guide was published. The following Japanese sources were used for reference in editing Genichi's bequeathed fragments and complementing his translations:

- J.1 Inoue Enryō 井上圓了.「哲學堂の記」[Record of the Philosophy Shrine],『東洋哲學』[Oriental philosophy] vol. 11, no. 8 (September 1904).
- J.2 Inoue Enryō 井上圓了.『哲界一瞥』[A glance at the world of philosophy] (1913). Reprinted in vol. 2, pp. 64–88 of『井上円了選集』[Inoue Enryō selected writings], pub. by Toyo University 東洋大学 (1987–2004).
- J.3 Inoue Enryō 井上圓了.「哲學上に於ける余の使命」[My philosophical mission],『東洋哲學』[Eastern Philosophy] vol. 26, no. 2 (February 1919): pp. 83–93.
- J.4 Inoue Enryō 井上圓了.『哲學堂案内』[Guide to the Philosophy Shrine], 3rd rev. and enlarged ed. by Inoue Genichi 井上玄一, pub. by "Philosophy Shrine Foundation" 財団法人哲學堂 (1920).
- J.5 Ishikawa Gishō 石川義昌, ed.『哲學堂』[The Philosophy Shrine], pub. by "Philosophy Shrine Foundation" 財団法人哲學堂 (1941).
- J.6 Inoue Genichi 井上玄一.「英文哲学堂案内：邦文概説及び備考」[English guide to the Philosophy Shrine: Outline and notes in

Japanese], 37 pages, extra print pub. by "Research Unit of the Founder of Toyo University" 東洋大学学祖研究室 (Nov. 1962). Original held by Inoue Enryo Research Center.

J.7 Inoue Genichi 井上玄一.『哲学堂案内』[Guide to the Philosophy Shrine], pub. by "Association for the Promotion of the Philosophy Shrine" 哲学堂宣揚会 (1968).

The principles according to which this Guide was edited can be named as follows:

a) Faithfulness to Enryō's ideas and explanations as seen in materials J.1 to J.4.
b) Faithfulness to names and inscriptions in the Garden and surroundings.
c) Faithfulness to historical truth.
d) Use of Genichi's drafts as preserved in materials E.1 to E.4.
e) Contemporary usability.

These principles collided in many ways. First of all, Genichi's translations are rather free, sometimes distorting, and, in some instances, wrong. The principle of making as much use as possible of Genichi's preliminary work (d) therefore collided with the principle of faithfulness to the Japanese source materials (a). These two editorial principles collided even more so in cases where Genichi deliberately corrected, modified, or extended the Japanese sources, as he particularly did in the chapters that became Part II of this edition. Genichi wanted to update Enryō's introductions of the sages according to more recent research. He himself therefore applied principles (c) and (e). While editing Part II, I followed Genichi in applying these principles by adding further reading recommendations and by omitting some outright misleading information—one striking example of which is Enryō's statement that Socrates did not even attempt to defend himself before drinking the poison (cf. J.2, IS 2:76). Despite such revision of contents by Genichi and myself in Part II, Part I of the Guide nevertheless contains a complete and fairly faithful translation of J.4.

Genichi's Prefaces are the most refined English materials he bequeathed, and needed little editorial work. The Afterword was not written by Genichi in the way it is presented here—only the last paragraph was intended to be part of an epilogue. The other pieces of the text were collected by me from source E.4, in order to rescue more of Genichi's work (d). The overall arrangement of the materials likewise does not follow Genichi's original scheme. Genichi wanted to integrate the introductory chapters about the sages into the main body of the text, as was done in J.5 by Ishikawa Gishō. Other parts, such as the description of Enryō's tomb, translations of related verses, etc. (which Genichi planned to compile as the second and third parts of the Guide), have been collected in the Appendix. The chart below lists for each chapter the author of the originally Japanese text, the Japanese source materials, the author or translator of the English text as well as the English source materials. Names of authors and translators are given by their initials.

Contents	Jap. Author	Jap. Source	Eng. Translator	Eng. Source
Introduction	I.G.	J.6, J.7	I.G.	E.2, E.3
Preface	I.G.	J.7	I.G.	E.2
I. Guide to the Temple Garden of Philosophy				
1. Introductory Remarks	I.E.	J.4	R.S.	
2. Entrance Section	I.E.	J.4	R.S.	

3. Skull Hermitage	I.E.	J.4	R.S.	
4. Shrine of the Four Sages	I.E.	J.4	R.S.	
5. Ceiling of the Shrine	I.E.	J.4	R.S.	
6. Selection of the Four Sages	I.E.	J.4	I.G.	E.1
7. Mantra Pillar	I.E.	J.4, tablet	I.G.	E.1
8. Pagoda of the Six Wise Men	I.E.	J.4	I.G.	E.1
9. Route to Garden of Materialism	I.E.	J.4	I.G.	E.1
10. Garden of Materialism	I.E.	J.4	I.G.	E.1
11. Route to Garden of Idealism	I.E.	J.4	I.G.	E.1
12. Garden of Idealism	I.E.	J.4	I.G.	E.1
13. Domain of Logic	I.E.	J.4	I.G.	E.1
14. Citadel of the Absolute	I.E.	J.4 (63) (66)	R.S.	
15. Rear Gate	I.E.	J.4	R.S.	
16. Universe Hall	I.E.	J.4 (74)	R.S.	
17. Three Erudites Arbor	I.E.	J.4	R.S.	
II. Introducing the World Sages				
1. Four Sages	I.E.	J.2, IS 2:73–77	I.G., R.S.	E.1
2. Six Wise Men	I.E.	J.2, IS 2:77–84	I.G., R.S.	E.1
3. Three Fathers	I.E.	(25) J.5	I.G., R.S.	E.1
4. Three Erudites	I.E.	J.2, IS 2:84–87	R.S.	
Afterword			I.G.	E.4

Appendix

A) 77 Features	I.E.	J.4	I.G., R.S.	E.1–4
B) Portrait	N.M.	scroll, IS 24:24	R.S.	
C) Eight Views	I.E.	J.1	I.G., R.S.	E.1
D) Hermit Life	I.E.	J.4, J.7	C.F.	E.1, E.3
E) My Mission	I.E.	J.3	I.G.	E.4
F) History		board	I.G., R.S.	E.4
G) Tomb	I.G., T.H.	tomb, J.4	I.G., R.S.	E.1, E.4

I.E.	Inoue Enryō	N.M.	Nakamura Masanao
I.G.	Inoue Genichi	T.H.	Tsuchiya Hiroshi
R.S.	Rainer Schulzer	C.F.	Charlotte Frietch

Enryō's playfulness with Chinese script—not only in the Garden, but also in the form of his tombstone—gives a hint to visitors about the most ingenious characteristic of his Garden: the interplay between that script and features of the Garden, between philosophical concepts and imagination, between poetry and visual art. Special attention therefore had to paid to the translations of names and inscriptions in the Garden (b). In order to compile a guide that is useful for contemporary tourists as well as for scholars, for reference I included every name, inscription, calligraphy, and verse in their exact Sino-Japanese character variants (e). Appendix A compares Genichi's and my translations of the 77 features of the Garden. In the main text, I consistently used the translation that I decided to be more adequate to the name and the respective garden feature. Consequently, I exchanged some of Genichi's translations with my renderings in the chapters Genichi translated, and *vice versa*. The chart below shows other translations of names and keywords that I standardized for this edition.

Name / Term	Reading	Trans. Genichi	Trans. Schulzer
道徳山哲學寺	*Dōtoku-san Tetsugaku-ji*	Temple of Philosophical Religion on the Hill of Morals	Philosophy Temple on Mount Morality
富士山	*Fuji-san*		Mount Prosperous Lord
武藏野	*Musashino*		Warrior Hide Plain
妙正寺川	*Myōshō-ji-gawa*		Temple River of Wondrous Uprightness
中野	*Nakano*		Midfield
南無絶對無限尊	*Namu Zettai-mugen-son*	Sacred Utterance: Absolute-Infinite-Supreme	Hail, Hallowed Infinite Absolute!
野方	*Nogata*		Fieldside
蓮華寺	*Renge-ji*		Lotus Flower Temple
四聖像	*Shisei-zō*		Portrait of the Four Sages
哲學堂	*Tetsugaku-dō*	Philosophy Shrine	Philosophy Hall
哲學堂八景	*Tetsugaku-dō hakkei*	Eight Views of the Temple-Garden	Eight Views around the Philosophy Shrine
哲學堂公園	*Tetsugaku-dō kōen*	Temple-Garden of Philosophy	Temple Garden of Philosophy
哲學堂際	*Tetsugaku-dō-sai*		Ceremony of the Philosophy Shrine

哲學館	*Tetsugaku-kan*	School of Philosophy	Philosophy Academy
哲學際	*Tetsugaku-sai*		Philosophy Ceremony
東洋大學	*Tōyō daigaku*	Oriental College	Toyo University
和田山	*Wada-yama*		Peaceful Paddy Hill

Enryō's Garden is not simply an isolated place with some curious names attached; it is imbedded in a culture of telling names and narrating landscapes. The significance of place names, which in other civilizations is forgotten due to phonetic shifting or semantic loss, is kept alive in East Asia due to the logographic character of the Chinese script. In East Asia, in addition to common names in landscape and human civilization being highly emblematic, in the scholarly traditions—particularly in Buddhism—the naming of persons, places, temples or artifacts is also a matter of symbolism, and it is given thoughtful consideration. *Nomen est omen* is the maxim according to which such nomenclature should be interpreted. Because of the cultural significance of the Chinese script, Enryō opposed the abolishment of Chinese characters that was being debated towards end of the nineteenth century. To underline his point, Enryō even proposed a form of "education by naming" 名稱教育 (IS 2: 404–10), which became part of the theory behind his Garden. Rendering all places, names, imperial eras, and Buddhist names into English is uncommon, primarily because translations become awkward. However, for the reasons given above, a different approach was experimentally adopted here, particularly in editing Appendix C. *The Eight Views around the Philosophy Shrine* are Enryō's attempt to stimulate a romantic sense of the beauty of nature through education by naming. By learning that the Philosophy Garden lies in the Warrior Hide Plain of the Eastern Capital, alongside the Temple River of Wondrous Uprightness, visitors may get a taste of the poetic worldview the Chinese script affords.

It would be tedious to go into more detail about the many decisions I had to make in order to balance the editorial principles given above. All in all, I did not handle the source materials as a philologist, but as an editor who is interested in publishing a useful handbook for exploring the Garden (e). I believe this to reflect the best of Enryō's intentions. The Temple Garden of Philosophy embodies Enryō's vision of a "natural education" 自然教育 that proceeds by reading the "living book of heaven and earth" 天地の活書, as opposed to "dead learning" 死學 from books (IS 2: 324-28). Enryō surely would have given primacy to the usability of the guidebook over philological detail with an overload of footnotes.

Illustrations

Literature

Bodiford, William. "Inoue Enryo in Retirement: Philosophy as Spiritual Cultivation," *International Inoue Enryo Research* 2 (2014): 19-54.

Ideno Naoki 出野尚紀.「哲学堂八景」[The eight views around the Philosophy Shrine], *Annual Report of the Inoue Enryo Center* 20 (2011): 119–46.

———.「哲学堂開園までの公園様相」[Characteristics of parks until the opening of the Philosophy Shrine garden], *Annual Report of the Inoue Enryo Center* 21 (2012): 87–116.

Inoue Enryō 井上圓了.『井上円了選集』[Inoue Enryō selected writings], abbr. IS (Tokyo: 東洋大学, 1987–2004).

———. "My Philosophical Mission" (1919), trans. by Dylan Luers Toda, *International Inoue Enryo Research* 3 (2015): 42–49.

Maejima Yasuhiko 前地康彦.『哲学堂公園』, pub. by 東京都公園協会監修 (Tokyo: 郷学舎, 1980) (東京公園文庫 21).

Miura Setsuo 三浦節夫.「井上円了と哲学堂公園一〇〇年」[Inoue Enryō and one hundred years Temple Garden of Philosophy], *Annual Report of the Inoue Enryo Center* 11 (2002): 53–134.

Nakanoku Kyōiku Iinkai 中野区教育委員会, pub.「哲学堂公園内石造物及聯・扁額類調査報告書」[Research report about the carved stones, wooden tablets, etc. and their inscriptions in the Temple Garden of Philosophy],『中野の文化財』[Cultural properties of Nakano], no. 13 (1988).

TANAKA Junichirō 田中純一郎.「橋本雅邦《四聖像》考：井上円了思想とその絵画化について」[Examining Hashimoto Gahō's 'Picture of the Four Sages': Inoue Enryō's thought and it's visualization], *The Journal of Art Studies*『美術研究』424 (2018): 564–82.
Tōyō Daigaku Fuzoku Toshokan 東洋大学付属図書館, pub.『哲學堂圖書館圖書目錄』[Catalog of the Philosophy Shrine Library] [1916] (Tokyo: 東洋大学, 1985).

About the Editor

Rainer Schulzer, Associate Professor of Philosophy (PhD), Member of Faculty of Information Networking for Innovation and Design, Toyo University

Rainer Schulzer studied philosophy, Japanese studies and Chinese studies at Humboldt University of Berlin, where he received a doctoral degree in philosophy in 2012. His dissertation, *Inoue Enryō: A Philosophical Portrait*, was published by SUNY Press in 2019. His research fields are comparative philosophy, ethical theory, and philosophical anthropology.

Guide to the Temple Garden of Philosophy

2019年8月30日　初版発行

著作者　Rainer Schulzer

発行所　東洋大学出版会
〒112-8606　東京都文京区白山5-28-20
電話（03）3945-7563
http://www.toyo.ac.jp/site/toyo-up/
発売所　丸善出版株式会社
〒101-0051　東京都千代田区神田神保町二丁目17番
電話（03）3512-3256
https://www.maruzen-publishing.co.jp

組版　株式会社オメガ・コミュニケーションズ
印刷・製本　大日本印刷株式会社
ISBN　978-4-908590-07-8　C3025